Being Presbyterian in the Bible Belt

Being Presbyterian in the Bible Belt

A THEOLOGICAL SURVIVAL GUIDE FOR YOUTH, PARENTS, AND OTHER CONFUSED PRESBYTERIANS

Ted V. Foote Jr.
P. Alex Thornburg

Geneva Press
Louisville, Kentucky

Scripture quotations from the New Revised Standard Version of the Bible are copyright © 1989 by the Division of Christian Education of the National Council of the Churches of Christ in the U.S.A. and are used by permission.

Cover design, book design, and illustration by Rohani Design, Edmonds, Washington

First edition

Published by Geneva Press
Louisville, Kentucky

This book is printed on acid-free paper that meets the American National Standards Institute Z39.48 standard. ∞

PRINTED IN THE UNITED STATES OF AMERICA

01 02 03 04 05 06 07 08 09 — 10 9 8 7 6 5

Library of Congress Cataloging-in-Publication Data

Foote, Ted V., 1953–
  Being Presbyterian in the Bible belt : a theological survival guide for youth, parents, and other confused Presbyterians / Ted V. Foote, Jr., P. Alex Thornburg.
    p. cm
  Includes bibliographical references.
  ISBN 0-664-50109-5 (alk. paper)
  1. Presbyterian Church—Apologetic works. 2. Fundamentalism. 3. Evangelicalism. I. Thornburg, P. Alex, 1960– II. Title.
BX9175.2 .F66 2000
285'.1—dc21

99-088569

Contents

To
Teresa and Joanie,
Noah, Emma, Kendall, and Payton,
and to all across the centuries who have both
been sought by and been seeking the God of grace.

Preface

In 1955 one of us was almost two years old and the other was "not yet" by a handful of years. That year Westminster Press published Robert McAfee Brown's *The Bible Speaks to You,* a book with a respectful, holy, and appropriate sense of humor about human nature and the Bible. Brown hoped to assist high school and college age youth, young adults, and anyone else reading the Bible toward an awareness of how modern critical scholarship, sound biblical interpretation, and contemporary life intersect. His treatment of the power and promise of the Bible can be read and studied again and again.

When Dr. Brown wrote *The Bible Speaks to You* forty-five years ago, he was aware of a conflict between "fundamentalist" and "liberal" schools of interpretation. Finding neither school completely helpful for living out one's faith, Brown attempted to assist his readers in walking a different, "third route" in their journeys of biblical interpretation and theological and spiritual growth.

Since that time, when Dwight Eisenhower was president of the United States, the church and culture have changed some, to say the least. Now the broad mainline theological perspective from which Brown wrote is very much a minority perspective on a religious landscape dominated by other viewpoints. These other theological perspectives promote their own "majority views" on the faith with such energy, enthusiasm, and media visibility that youth and adults seeking "another way" may not even know other ways exist.

The Presbyterian Church (U.S.A.) is aware of the challenge to articulate its theology to a new generation. In 1998 the General Assembly approved a set of catechisms for use by children, youth, and adults. The effort poured into the catechism project and the contribution it makes to faith education are developments we applaud. Even so, we believe that more is still needed by disciples, younger and older. If the catechisms help provide a foundation and a framework for a person's house of faith, we hope this book will help readers think through how this house can be furnished and arranged. Catechisms are for insiders; they give answers to faith questions we Presbyterians ask ourselves. In this "survival guide" we hope to do the opposite: to respond to "outsiders," to address the questions non-Presbyterians ask us.

However, this is no book of easy answers. It is, rather, an effort to hear the religious questions people ask Presbyterians, to interpret those questions, and to explore how Presbyterians can respond out of the richness and the depth of both the Bible and our Reformed and Presbyterian faith tradition. We hope these chapters make some contribution to the quest for Presbyterians to live faithfully and joyfully in service to the Lord of heaven and earth. Other ways of seeing and living the Christian faith are worthy and blessed by God, yet we are unapologetic about the Reformed and Presbyterian tradition, having been strengthened by it ourselves and confident that others may be also.

The debt of gratitude we owe to family, mentors, fellow disciples, and life-pilgrims older and younger, as well as the editorial team at Geneva Press, is surpassed only by the debt of gratitude we owe to God. Living with and among congregations we have served has shaped many of our insights about the Reformed faith. Additionally, we have truly learned what it means to be Presbyterian in the Bible Belt from congregations in Tulsa, Owasso, and Stillwater, Oklahoma, and in Dallas, Gatesville, Waco, Austin, Pasadena, San Antonio, Henderson, and Rusk County, Texas. Of course, any shortcomings or errors found in these pages are attributable only to the two of us.

God began a conversation with God's people long before any of us were ever conceived. We hope and pray this volume will make a contribution to that ages-long conversation to the end that we may more clearly discern the grace surrounding us all. With humility and boldness rooted in God's grace, we count it a privilege to be engaged in dialogue with those who read these pages.

Sola Gloria Dei,

P. Alex Thornburg   Ted V. Foote, Jr.

Introduction

Being Presbyterian in the Bible Belt (and Elsewhere)

> ### Entering the Bible Belt
> ### Not a region
> ### but a state of mind

- Tina, a fifteen-year-old, shares the experience of a close friend who constantly asked her, was she saved and, if so, had she been baptized as an adult? Her friend was scandalized and somewhat worried when she found out Tina had been baptized as a baby and couldn't give her a time and place when she "accepted Jesus as her personal Lord and Savior." "Don't you Presbyterians believe in being saved?" her friend asked. Tina was confused, upset, and angry. She knew she didn't believe what her friend was saying, but she couldn't articulate what she really believed.

> *"You Presbyterians are the problem."*
>
> —*Andrew Young* [1]

- An upset mother calls her pastor because her son has been going to another church's youth group and has come home wrestling with questions she doesn't know how to answer. He's told her, "Mom, they want me to be baptized and immersed. They say I won't go to heaven unless I do. They even say unless I get you to come to their church, you aren't saved either." The mother doesn't know how to respond and asks the pastor what she should do.

• A Presbyterian church member struggles to explain to his neighbor what he, as a Presbyterian, believes about the biblical book of Revelation. "Will you be taken up in the rapture?" his neighbor asks. "Taken where?" the church member says aloud. The next Sunday the member asks his pastor if they could do a study on the book of Revelation. "Maybe in the third millennium," the pastor says.

When was I saved? Do we believe in the rapture? Do we believe some people are going to hell? Do we believe the Bible is literally true? These are some of the questions Presbyterians have been asking over the years, questions often first posed to them by friends who come from fundamentalist churches.

While the issues examined in the following pages are matters that cross all sorts of lines (geographic, ideological, and generational), this book arises out of our experiences as ministers who live and preach in the Bible Belt—which is not so much a place as it is a state of mind. These chapters reflect our personal journeys of faith and discovery in that particular brand of Christianity called Presbyterian. Obviously, we also believe the issues we continue to struggle with in this book also reflect the questions many of you face in everyday life.

We have listened to many members, young and old, strive to understand what it means to call ourselves Presbyterian. This question becomes especially acute when we find ourselves in dialogue with fundamentalist Christian perspectives. To live in the Bible Belt (and elsewhere) is to find oneself in conversation with people who have no idea what Presbyterians believe, or why. The problem, of course, is that often we don't really know how to express what we believe either. We hope and intend that this book will address that challenge.

THE FREEDOM IN BEING A MINORITY IN A BIBLE BELT CULTURE

It wasn't too long ago that the majority of Christians in the United States identified themselves with what are called "mainline traditional churches," which customarily means Methodist, Episcopal, United Church of Christ, Lutheran, Disciples of Christ, and Presbyterians. In the early part of this century, to be Christian was essentially to worship in one of these traditions. The larger churches in many communities were part of these traditions. One was a Presbyterian because one's parents were Presbyterian, and to be Presbyterian was to be part of a majority in society, part of the establishment. Being Presbyterian was unquestioned—or, at least, the questions were less pressing—because we were the *norm* as mainline Christians and not the *exception*.

Increasingly, this is no longer true. To be Presbyterian today is to be part of a minority. A greater number of Christians in the United States today identify themselves with more conservative, neo-evangelical[2] theological traditions. The larger churches are no longer "mainline" but megachurches that emphasize a particular slant on scripture, namely an emphasis on saving lost souls. Presbyterians no longer represent the Christian norm; neo-evangelicals do. Moreover, in addition to the neo-evangelical Christian majority, there are also more Muslims in the United States than there are Presbyterians at this time.[3] To be Presbyterian is no longer to be assured of being part of the "in-church" people are expected to attend.

This is not necessarily a bad thing. While numerical losses in member-ship can surely be disconcerting, at the same time we are now free to embrace our belief not because it is what our parents believed or because the majority of Americans hold our view, but because it best expresses our experience of God. To be Presbyterian today is to *decide* to claim those core affirmations that make us Presbyterian. While Presbyterians may not have the political and financial clout we once had, we have something far more important: a liberating understanding of the gospel. We can claim this gospel as a minority community seeking to be faithful to our calling rather than as part of the majority opinion. We can learn much from other minorities (such as the Jewish community) who have held on to their core beliefs and values in the face of a dominant culture. Being part of a minor-ity requires us to examine our basic beliefs, particularly as such beliefs come into conversation and even conflict with more dominant viewpoints. The good news is that God has a tendency to speak through minority view-points.[4] God is funny that way!

THE IMPORTANCE IN BEING A CONFESSING CHURCH

Why is it so important for us to be able to know and to say what we believe as Presbyterian? First, we understand ourselves to be part of a confessing church. This means that the way we speak of our faith has a *history*, and we join with other Christians in affirming the confessions of faith Christians have made down through the ages (such as the Apostles' Creed). However, it also means that is important to be able to confess the faith *today*, to affirm in this new time and place all those historic creeds as our own. The Presbyterian Church (U.S.A.) *Book of Confessions* contains confessions that come all the way from the early days of the church (the Apostles' Creed) to our own time (A Brief Statement of Faith, 1991). Each of these confessions represents an attempt to articulate the basic nucleus of the faith in light of some new circumstance or conflict in history. To be a confessing church is to take a stand and state what we believe. This is part of what being Presbyterian is about.

Second, it is important to confess our faith because of the uncertainty of our world today. With the variety of beliefs and claims to truth in our amazingly small world, there is much ambivalence about what exactly to believe. There are many who even give up believing in anything. In this time of uncertainty and disbelief, it is our task as one part of our Lord's church to share with the world what we believe and why. We do this with humility and respect for other beliefs. (See the last chapter for why this is.) One of the statements of faith in the Presbyterian *Book of Confessions* is called The Theological Declaration of Barmen.[5] This confession came out of the church in Germany during the 1930s as the Nazi party began to take over all aspects of German society, including the church. A minority (there's that word again) of churches came together and made a short affirmation of faith: "Jesus Christ is Lord." Not Hitler, not the Nazi party, not any particular political perspective—nothing takes precedence over that truth. Only Christ is the head of the church, and only Christ is ultimately to be obeyed. These are dangerous views in a world in which affirming them might get you killed.[6]

Moreover, how Jesus is understood becomes an issue in such a debate. Professor Karl Barth, teaching in Germany in 1934, preached a sermon on December 10 wherein he stated emphatically, "Jesus Christ was a Jew." Some left the church during the sermon in protest.[7] One wonders, if more preachers had confessed this truth, how different history might have been.

Can you see now how important it can be to state what you believe?

THERE BE DRAGONS HERE

There are some dangers we face here. First, we will be talking about faith views and doing theology together, and this is not easy or safe work. Presbyterians often fervently disagree on issues (which is part of the fun of being Presbyterian!), and we are aware of how risky it is to try to speak for all Presbyterians, to attempt to say clearly what we hold in common. You may even disagree with some things written in this book. We hope so, since the very fact of your disagreement would mean that you are using the brain God gave you and expects you to use.[8] Still, we passionately believe Presbyterians have a vital message to bring to the world today, and we want to try to give voice to the basic beliefs of Presbyterians and to affirm our theological tradition.

Another danger in this book is that some readers may think that we are engaging in fundamentalist bashing. To be sure, we are writing out of the conviction that much of what is communicated to our culture as the Christian message is distorted and misleading. Much of what certain Christians claim to be "true" is, we would argue, unbiblical. Therefore, we *are* attempting to articulate basic Presbyterian beliefs in conversation with those who espouse a more fundamentalist perspective of our faith, fully aware that their perspective tends to dominate the religious discussion in our present society. We answer the questions asked by others with what we believe to be Presbyterian answers. But to "bash" other Christians would itself be un-Presbyterian. We believe our brothers and sisters of the neo-evangelical tradition have much to teach us in our conversations. Their contribution to the shaping of our understanding of the mystery of God is valuable too.

Presbyterians have always understood themselves as one particular expression of a much larger church, one faith community among many. This is why the Presbyterian Church has embraced the ecumenical movement and affirms attempts to support the unity of the whole church. That is why we accept other churches' baptisms (Presbyterians don't ask Christians who come to us from another denomination to get rebaptized.), and we recognize other denominations as equal partners in doing the work of God's kingdom. The church belongs to Jesus Christ and not to Presbyterians or Baptists or Methodists or Pentecostals. Jesus is Lord, and no one else! (Do you recognize that confession?)

We Presbyterians approach any statements about God with humility. Why? Because, at heart, God is a mystery. The mystery of God cannot be explained or wrapped up neatly in a package of words. Indeed, much of our disagreement with fundamentalists is over their tendency to try to make the faith logically airtight and to claim "truth" exclusively as their own.

This book will engage such a closed view of truth and will present a way to express your faith in the light of the Reformed and Presbyterian understanding of God. Our purpose is not to denounce the beliefs of others but to provide for Presbyterians a way to respond to the questions of others that allows all to grow from the experience.

God alone is Lord of the conscience.[9] This is a statement we Presbyterians hold dear. No other authority, no other claim on our conscience, can be made than our own understanding of God's will for each of us individually. We respect each other's unique relationship with the living God, who gives guidance for our choices and decisions in life. On one level, this is why we Presbyterians can choose to dance, or to smoke, or to drink.[10] God rules your conscience and not anyone else. On another level, this statement is also an affirmation about one's own theological understandings. We believe it is important for all people to share their theological beliefs about God with the church. And the church is made richer for the variety of viewpoints of every person.

The danger, of course, is that we can conclude being Presbyterians means "anything goes." This is far from the truth. Another saying in our tradition is that "truth is in order to goodness."[11] Truth always bears the fruits of holiness, compassion, and justice. We measure all our theological statements on the unique and authoritative witness[12] to God in Jesus Christ. Scripture is our source and guide as we explore theology and the practice of faith. But while there are those who would make a prison of the Bible, we believe it to be liberating and freeing. (See chapter 2 on "scripture" to find out why.)

This book, in its own way, is a theological book, and theology is a community-centered exercise. As we have said: God alone is Lord of the conscience. But this does not mean that our faith is a lonely, individualistic quest. Theology is done best not by individuals but by a community of people: who pledge faithfulness to God; who struggle together to speak the truth as each understands it; and who listen to the truth others speak. This is why we decided to write this book together, as a team. We believe that it will be a better theological book because we do it as coauthors. In our discussions, entailing many times of agreement and also a little bit of argument, we have been mutually enriched, and the book, we are convinced, has been made better by this give and take. Ultimately, two heads are better than one (unless you are in a horror movie), and we would encourage you to discuss some of the ideas of this book with others. The ultimate risk of doing theology is being part of a community where God constantly surprises us with new angles to God's truth.

GRACE IS THE KEY WORD

You will find through each of the chapters in this book that basically we are describing grace. Grace is radical. It is at the root of all we do and say as Presbyterians. From questions about our salvation, to questions about heaven, to questions about faith and community and mission, grace is the framework undergirding all our belief. Ultimately, grace is also what creates a different flavor in Presbyterian beliefs and theology from the beliefs and theology of many around us. If you get nothing else out of this book, we hope you will understand just how special the grace of God is in Jesus Christ. As you read along, always remember: Grace is the word!

WHAT IS GRACE?

At the heart of the Presbyterian understanding of God is one thing: grace! Grace is God's love and acceptance freely given and not earned. Grace is a gift not to people who deserve it or to people because they are particularly special. It is a gift given out of the generosity of God's love for all creation. Grace is boundless and expansive, and, many believe, in the end, irresistible. Grace affirms that it is not humanity that saves itself but God, who has acted in the past, still acts today, and will act tomorrow. Grace is God's gift to undeserving children (regardless of each one's age!).

So What Do *You* Think?

1. Have you been asked any faith questions by fundamentalist Christians? If so, how did you feel about them? How did you respond to them? Has anyone ever implied that your beliefs were wrong or inferior? How did that feel? What did you do at that time or later?

2. Think about a situation in which you have experienced religious diversity (you were with others who have a different religion or different beliefs). Did this deepen or narrow your appreciation: (a) of them? (b) of life? (c) of your beliefs and identity? (d) of God?

3. Compose a brief creative essay, write a poem or song, or draw a sketch that expresses your experience of "faith born of grace."

Are You Saved, or Are You Presbyterian?

WHEN WERE YOU SAVED?

"I was saved around two thousand years ago." When Presbyterians respond this way to a question we hear often in the Bible Belt—"When were you saved?"—it reflects our conviction that salvation is centered in the life, death, and resurrection of Jesus two millennia ago. When a neo-evangelical asks when you were saved, however, they are focused not on what Jesus did long ago but on your present religious experience—the year, the day, the moment when you "accept Jesus" into

Warning: Grace Abounds

your life. Often for the neo-evangelical, you are not actually saved unless you are able to cite the particular day and time when this acceptance occurred. This is why the question is so important to them and their system of belief. If you don't know, then "where will you go?"

Since, for the neo-evangelical Christian in the Bible Belt, the significant event in a Christian's salvation is this moment of acceptance or conversion, opportunities to come forward in church and to commit one's life to Jesus are central to worship. Mission is focused on bringing people to Christ through preaching, convicting people of their sin, and helping them accept Christ into their hearts. Life in the church is shaped by this important task of helping more and more people find their salvation.

There is a sense of urgency for the neo-evangelicals as they seek to bring more and more people to Christ. If they don't ask you, if they don't try to bring you to Jesus, then your soul is at stake. When many youth share a sense of frustration about friends who push them on this question, it should be understood that, for the neo-evangelical, another's salvation is in limbo unless one can give a particular answer. Without that verbal accept-ance, without that sense of the moment when you accepted Jesus Christ, without that conversion, you will "go to hell." With this theology, all things take a back seat to this task: "saving souls" for Jesus. "When were you saved?" becomes the most important question in the world.

A FEARFUL FUNERAL

A number of years ago, a teenager was killed in a car accident. The funeral was filled with high school friends and families as they mourned the death of a friend. The preacher emphasized to the congregation that it was good that the young man had accepted Christ into his life so that he was assured he would get into heaven. The preacher then proceeded to ask the congregation if each one had accepted Jesus Christ into her or his heart, because "you never know if your life could end in one split second just as suddenly as this young man's." Fear seemed to be reflected in the eyes of a number of the young people. Do you wonder how, in the midst of such grief and tragedy, the preacher could use this funeral as a way to bring people to Jesus even through fear? Yet for that preacher, this especially is a time to "get people saved," because the possibil-ity of losing a soul could have eternal ramifications. In his mind, converting people to Christ is most important. Everything else takes a back seat.

DO PRESBYTERIANS BELIEVE IN CONVERSION?

"I was saved two thousand years ago." What do we mean by this statement? First of all, we are affirming that our salvation is not dependent on one particular moment when we accepted Christ or one particular moment when we were converted. In fact, salvation is not something *we* do at all. It is *God* who acts; it is *God* who saves through Jesus Christ. We affirm, rather, that no moment of acceptance saves us, but God in Christ who acted yesterday, acts today, and will act tomorrow saves us. One key element of the Presbyterian tradition is a focus on God's saving action rather than human action. Our emphasis will always be on God who saves and redeems rather than our own words or actions in saving ourselves.

An interesting story in the Gospels (John 3:1–21) highlights this difference. In fact, this passage is often cited by neo-evangelicals when they talk about "being born again." The story is about Nicodemus, a Pharisee and leader of the Jews, who comes to Jesus under the cover of night. "Rabbi," he says, "we know you are a teacher who has come from God; for no one can do these signs that you do apart from the presence of God."

Jesus responds with some very strange words. (Jesus has a habit of saying strange things.) "Very truly, I tell you, no one can see the kingdom of God without being born from above." This phrase highlights the difficulty literalists have in trying to assert that we should take the Bible word for word. The Greek phrase popularly translated as "born again" or "born anew" is more literally translated "born from above." The "born again Christians" could be more truly be described as Christians "born from above."

Jesus' wording points to the truth that our ability to encounter the kingdom of God comes not from our human striving but from a birth granted by God from above.[1] To take this passage literally is to miss the whole point. To be "born from above"—poetically speaking—is to be born by God, shaped by God, converted by God. Problems arise when neo-evangelicals interpret this birth as a once-in-a-lifetime experience. That interpretation misunderstands Jesus' emphasis on God's actions and the continual process of being born from above. (For more on why literalism is unbiblical, see the next chapter.)

But Nicodemus asks Jesus, "How can anyone be born after having grown old? Can anyone enter a second time into the mother's womb and be born?" Nicodemus would have made a good literalist! Then Jesus responds with even stranger words. (There he goes again!) "Very truly, I tell you, no one can enter the kingdom of God without being born of water and Spirit. The wind blows where it chooses, and you hear the sound of it, but you do not know where it comes from or where it goes. So it is with everyone who is born of the Spirit." The birth into the kingdom is one of water (more on baptism later) and of the Spirit. And this Spirit (the Greek word for "wind" can also be translated as "Spirit") blows where it will. It comes and goes by God's hand and not by our human will. Jesus is saying that the birth from above is God's seemingly random action like the wind that blows where it chooses. To be born from above is to trust in God's

Spirit to save us as God is spiritually present in our physical lives. We do not, then, trust in our own abilities to save ourselves.

A little further in the John 3 discussion, Jesus speaks the words we have seen cited on more posters at football games than beer ads: "For *God* so loved the world that *God* gave the only Son so that everyone who believes in him may not perish but may have eternal life" (John 3:16, alt.; emphasis added). Notice that Jesus states it is God who loves the world; it is God who gave the Son. It is first and foremost God's actions that save and not our own. Jesus does point to the truth that believing is integral to this eternal life, but believing is not simply a kind of intellectual assent, a simple embrace of certain abstract truths. Again the Greek word is much richer in meaning than this. Believing is a deeper experience than simply answering an altar call, walking an aisle, and saying certain words. The word for believing implies trust, a living relationship of faith that is both intellectual and emotional. Trust is the ability to put one's faith not in ourselves but in another. "Trust in me," Jesus is saying, "and you will experience God's love and nearness."

The point is this: Presbyterians understand conversion to be a lifelong process. Trust isn't shared one time only, but continuously. Being "born again" is not a single event we necessarily point to and say, "That is when I was saved." There may be moments of God's presence that are particularly powerful in our lifelong conversion, but salvation is not dependent on them. To be "born from above" is a process whereby God shapes us more and more in the image of Christ. God is continually at work reforming us in God's image. Conversion is less about a particular time and place and more about lives lived in trust to a God who chooses us and who continuously loves us to wholeness. (The Greek word for "salvation" carries the meaning of "being made whole or complete.")

For many neo-evangelicals in the Bible Belt, salvation is dependent on that moment when you convert. For the Presbyterian, salvation is dependent on God who acted throughout Israel's history and in the life, death, and resurrection of Jesus Christ. This same God acts in our lives today and everyday. Salvation is a gift (grace!) given to us to be opened and celebrated not once but continuously as our lives are opened by God's gracious Spirit. Our task is to trust (believe) in that gift.

WHY DO WE BAPTIZE BABIES
(AND GOD'S CHILDREN OF ALL AGES)?

As we have seen, Presbyterians emphasize God's action over human action in salvation. This is why we baptize babies. Because we believe salvation is not initiated by our actions but, in fact, is God's gift to all, then baptizing a child affirms that God's grace comes to us long before we ever realize it. God is shaping our souls and lives, and sometimes we are not even aware of how God is involved in forming us into the people we are becoming. So, when we baptize a baby or person of any age, we believe (trust) that this child belongs to God and is being formed by God even without any visible signs of this forming.[2] The community of faith promises that this child will be raised in the faith and will experience the grace of God in their midst. When a child is baptized, the church promises to join with the parents in taking responsibility for the child's spiritual development. The baptism becomes a starting point rather than an end in itself—the beginning of a lifelong conversion to God's grace. The power of baptism is not tied to the moment when it is administered but only dramatizes the beginning of the journey bringing us deeper and deeper into Christ.

By contrast, for the neo-evangelical the emphasis is on the believer's actions, the believer's words and commitment, the believer's ability to embrace the faith. For Presbyterians, baptism is something "done for us" by God through the community of faith. It is about how God embraces us. This is why baptism is received only once in the Presbyterian Church. Our Directory of Worship states, "God's faithfulness needs no renewal."[3] We may need renewal and recommitment at times in our life. *We* may need to embrace God's love in a renewed way, but *God's* faithfulness to us does not need renewal. There is no need for repeated baptisms because God has claimed us once and for all as God's own in our baptism. What God has begun in our baptism, God faithfully continues throughout our lives. This is the truth we embrace as Presbyterians.

GRACE, NOT WORKS!

Consider this first-person testimony of grace:

I was like any normal twelve-year-old boy, which means I found plenty of opportunities to get into trouble. On one occasion, my best friend had come over to the house to spend the night, and like any normal twelve-year-old boys, we were a little rambunctious. My parents were going to a party across the alley and made a big deal about telling us that we were old enough to be left by ourselves for a little while. I remember my mother's parting words to us: "Now be good. Don't run around the house, and *don't break anything!*"

Being normal twelve-year-old boys, the first thing we did was to begin chasing each other through the house. At one point, as I ran from living room to dining room to kitchen with my friend trying to tackle me, I heard a crash in the dining room and my friend let out this frightful scream. To my horror, I saw that my mother's brand-new wooden dining room chair had been knocked over by one of us, and the top half had broken off. Fear and remorse seized us as we looked down on that broken chair. We then did what any normal twelve-year-old boys would do: we tried to cover it up.

I was rather ingenious at that age. I locked the door and sent my friend to get some glue out of a drawer, while I went into my parent's closet and got out some brown shoe polish and an old rag. We then glued the piece back onto the top of my mom's brand-new wooden dining room chair and, with the rag and shoe polish, tried to cover over the ragged crack.

At that point my mother, coming to check on us, knocked on the door and demanded to know why we had locked the door. We did what any normal twelve-year-old boys would do at this point: we panicked. I tried to hide the brown stained rag and glue in the utility room as my friend went to open the door. My mother came in and was immediately suspicious. "What's going on here?" she asked as she began to sniff the air.

Like any normal twelve-year-old boys we lied: "Nothing."

"Then why do you have brown shoe polish all over your hands?" she asked.

The jig was up. We then did what any normal twelve-year-old boys do in such instances: we blamed each other. "He did it!" we both said as we pointed our fingers at each other.

"Did what?" my mother said as I noticed her face getting redder and redder.

"Broke your brand-new wooden dining room chair," we shamefully responded expecting God's judgment to fall on us at any moment.

At this point my mother's eyes began to bulge, her lips were pressed tightly as if fire was trying to escape from her mouth, and we just knew she was about to explode. And she did explode—with peals of laughter. She laughed so hard, tears were rolling down her face. She laughed and laughed as she hugged both of us rather confused boys. I thought I had finally sent her over the edge into madness. Years later, she told me that what made her laugh was the brown shoe polish on our hands and faces looking so comical.

This was an experience of grace. Where we had expected harsh judgment and condemnation, we encountered laughter. Where we had thought there was no escape from the wrath about to fall on us, we instead were embraced in forgiveness. Grace is this experience of encountering God's laughter when we expect God's wrath. It is being embraced by God's love when we expect God's rejection of us. Grace is standing before God, our hands stained with our sin, and being washed clean by laughter, and hugs, and compassion.

This is the strange and mysterious nature of the God we believe in as Presbyterians. This is the God Jesus points to throughout his ministry and in his life. God's grace can be found in Jesus in countless ways, from the many times he sits to eat with tax collectors and prostitutes[4] to the story he told of a father who welcomes back a rebellious, prodigal son and throws a party for him, much to the chagrin of his other son.[5] The good news of Jesus Christ is that God's grace comes to us not because we have done anything to deserve it or because we are worthy of it. God's love and forgiveness come to us simply out of the boundless mercy of God's laughter.

This is good news to celebrate with other people. There is no more important message to bring to our culture than God's irresistible grace. Unfortunately, in our high schools and in our society, people are judged according to certain abilities and traits. If you "have what it takes," you increase the likelihood that you will succeed. If you say the right words, believe the right things, do the right actions, then you are deemed worthy of your peers' approval. Those in high school have the experience of seeing people judged and measured every day. How subtle, and sometimes not-so-subtle, the pressures are to fit into a certain mold so that we feel accepted and loved.

Grace teaches us that God loves us where we are and for who we are. Grace is knowing God loves us in the midst of our foolishness and power-lessness. Grace is experiencing God's laughter in our despair. The good news of grace is expressed fully in Paul's letter to the church in Rome. "For I am convinced that neither death, nor life, nor angels, nor rulers, nor things present, nor things to come, nor powers, nor height, nor depth, nor anything else in all creation, will be able to separate us from the love of God in Christ Jesus."[6] This is a rather remarkable thing to believe, is it not?

Finally, "grace without works is empty." We do not believe that our good deeds, our works, save us, even if one of those works is a coming forward during an altar call. Rather, we believe that when we experience grace, we are then led to do the good works expressive of that grace. Because I have experienced God's mercy, I can forgive another. Because God has welcomed me into the kingdom, I can welcome the stranger into my life. Because God loves the lost, I can seek the lost in our society and share God's love with them. Our works do not precede God's grace. They result from God's grace.

However, we should warn you: experiencing God's grace means being changed. Experiencing God's grace is to hear laughter where others only expect judgment. It is to experience God's embrace where others preach only God's condemnation. It is to look at the world very differently from some of our brothers and sisters. The world needs people changed by God's grace. The world needs people less concerned with their own personal salvation and more concerned with sharing God's grace. This is our job as Presbyterians. We were saved a long time ago, and we are saved every day and we will be saved in the future. Grace is our Word—a good one too.

So What Do *You* Think?

1. Think of your life and/or the life of someone you know. Describe how God's Spirit, in some way and at some time or times, has created new life "from above."

2. Describe various baptisms you've seen or heard about. Were there differences? Similarities? Was there anything moving about any of them? Ho-hum?

3. Imagine that you are Nicodemus (or some other biblical character of your choosing). Now, say or write how the following statement is true for you: "Grace is knowing God loves me in spite of myself." Now, drop the disguise and be yourself. How is the statement true for the real you?

Is the Bible the Literal Word of God, or Just a Long, Boring Book?

DO YOU BELIEVE IN THE BIBLE?

TROUBLED SLEEP

In a conversation at a sleepover with girlfriends, Jamie, a fifteen-year-old Presbyterian, hears Ellen say, "The youth pastor at my church says people who talk about the Bible not being true in every part are really not Christians." Jamie thinks of herself as a Christian, but she begins to wonder. She wonders what her mother, a Presbyterian elder, believes about this and what her pastor would have to say.

Of all the questions asked today of Presbyterians, several of which are discussed in this book, "Do you believe in the Bible?" may be the trickiest. It is the one most open to misinterpretation. The quick answer is: "No, most Presbyterians do not *believe in* the Bible. We *believe in* the Lord of heaven and earth." Obviously, that could provoke the astonished reply: "What? You don't believe in the Bible?" We would respond, yes, we don't believe in the Bible; we believe in God. We don't rest our faith in a *book*, but in *God's living presence*—a presence we discern in Israel's history and see completely revealed in the Jewish teacher, healer, and prophet named Jesus. Thus, we are making a distinction here: truth is not captured in the words on a page of the Bible but is the living Word who encounters us in those pages. (More about this later in this chapter!)

So, let's ask the big question: Do Presbyterians believe the Bible is the literal Word of God? This question cannot be answered simply. We Presbyterians are (and have been) a cantankerous group who enjoy good debates, particularly about the Bible. There is no doubt that Presbyterians (like people in other faith-traditions) believe differently among themselves about the Bible, about interpretations of Bible passages, and about almost any other subject you can think of. The joke is that when you get five Presbyterians together, you have eight different interpretations of a Bible passage!

Jesus was not a literalist

Presbyterian history reflects this debate, and there have been Presbyterians down through the years who have believed that the words of the Bible were literally God's words. Many Presbyterians through the generations have said something like "Yes, I believe the Bible is the literal Word of God." At least as far back as 1675, a Reformed gathering in Switzerland adopted a statement called the Helvetic Consensus Formula. (You could impress your friends throwing this into a conversation!) It stated that everything about the Bible is inspired—even the tiny vowel markings that later scholars added to the Hebrew words in the First (Old) Testament. The Bible, according to the the Helvetic Consensus Formula, is "the sole and complete rule of our faith and life."[1] Phrased another way, every word in the Bible can be trusted and is to be accepted as God's truth. The folk who created this statement believed that God inspired the writers even in the smallest details, and there are people today who still believe that God can be found in such details.

You sometimes hear people use the word "inerrant" to describe this view of the Bible as inspired even in its smallest details. You may hear others describe themselves as believing in "the inerrant truth of the Bible." Those who hold such inerrancy views argue that the Bible is absolutely true in every respect and without errors of any kind (not only errors of faith, but errors of science, math, and geography too). Inerrantists are one part of a larger group of Protestant fundamentalists who believe that the Bible expresses certain fundamental, inalterable, undeniable truths central to belief.

Our church has a long history of wrestling with this understanding of the Bible as inerrant. In both Scotland and the United States during the nineteenth and twentieth centuries, divisions developed among Presbyterians based on whether the Presbyterian Church would be guided by a fundamentalism of the "inerrancy school." As you might guess, heated arguments, heresy trials, and splits between inerrantists and noninerrantists resulted.[2] Presbyterians love to argue, especially about the Bible.

The tendency of Presbyterians to disagree about the Bible continues today, and many of our disputes about certain issues are essentially a result of differing interpretations of scriptures. Yet, even if Presbyterians have different ways of interpreting the Bible, it is central to the beliefs of all Presbyterians that the Bible is crucial to our practice of faith and understanding of God. We believe the "Scriptures of the Old and New Testaments to be, by the Holy Spirit, the unique and authoritative witness to Jesus Christ in the Church universal, and God's Word to you."[3] So while we may not always agree on particular interpretations, Presbyterians hold the Bible to be central for the discernment of God's will among us. Not only do Presbyterians love to argue, they love to find ways to accept their differences and find what it is we hold in common. The centrality of the Bible is one of those commonalities.

In our view, the problem with many inerrantists, literalists, and fundamentalists is that they claim a particular interpretation to be above all other interpretations. If someone truly took the Bible literally and did everything scripture passages call for, then they would not be eating pork (Leviticus 11:7), wearing certain kinds of clothing (Deuteronomy 22:11), or lending money to people and charging interest (Exodus 22:25). (Banks may not like this biblical teaching!) No one follows every part of the Bible literally, because no one does everything the Bible calls people to do. If we did, we'd be encouraging the cutting out of people's eyes for looking at the cover of the *Sports Illustrated* swimsuit issue (Matthew 5:28–29), and people would be selling everything they own to follow Jesus (Luke 18:22). There is no such thing as a purely literal interpretation of the Bible! Everyone makes choices about what to believe as true in the Bible and what is fundamental in following Jesus. The problem with literalists and fundamentalists is their claim that their interpretations are the only valid ones.

Inerrancy has other problems as well. If some want to argue that the Bible is true in all details, then what do they do with the fact that the earth is not flat or with the notion that heaven exists above the clouds and hell below in the center of the earth? To believe the Bible is true in all details is to assert that epilepsy is caused by demons, and the earth was made in seven twenty-four-hour periods. While some people may want to believe these things to be literally true, science and common sense show us that the Bible cannot be true in all of its particular details. (You can lose God in the details if you are not careful.)

On occasion, the Bible includes words in one place that are at variance or in conflict with what the Bible says elsewhere. For example, Genesis 1:26–28 teaches that human beings were created male and female at once, after the other creatures, but Genesis 2:7 and 2:18–23 teach that the order was human male, then the creatures, and then human female. Also, the book of Ezra clearly opposes the marriage of Jews who returned from exile in Babylon to the Palestinians whose ancestors were not carried into exile (Ezra 10:9–18). The book of Ruth, in contrast, chronicles the marriage of a Judean Jew named Boaz to a Moabite woman named Ruth, a marriage that was part of the family tree of King David (Ruth 4:18–22) and of Jesus (Matthew 1:5–6, 16).

So in answer to the question about whether Presbyterians believe the Bible to be the literal Word of God, we would respond, "No, because no one *really* believes in the Bible literally." Some may assert one interpretation over another; they may want to argue the world was made in seven days; and they may want to ignore the obvious contradictions in the Bible; but no one takes the Bible literally all the time! Those who argue for literalism, and who believe in it, worry that if there is not one correct interpretation, then "anything goes" as far as interpreting the Bible is concerned. And the church in the past has used the Bible to argue for just about anything from slavery[4] to denying women ordination as church officers.[5] More often than not, a particular interpretation reflects the biases and cultural prejudices of anyone who is an interpreter.

One example of this is the element within the Gospels we could describe as anti-Jewish. Two Gospel accounts—Matthew's and John's—strongly blame Jewish officials and, to some extent, Jewish people in general for being too much under the influence of Jewish religious leaders who, it is alleged, conspired to engineer Jesus' arrest and cruel death by crucifixion (Matthew 26:3–4; 27:25; John 11:47–53; 19:12–16). That's the angle that has provided a "biblical" rationale for anti-Semitism across the centuries. Anti-Semitism labels Jewish people as "Christ-killers." It cannot be said long enough or loudly enough that this interpretation and rationale are wrong! To articulate a biblical rationale for attacks on our Jewish brothers and sisters is a great misuse of scripture even though there are passages seemingly in support of this view. To say this is a truth for all time and places is to make prejudice a truth of certain writers in the first century. That prejudice, in fact, is untrue to the spirit and life of Jesus Christ.

Historically, of course, Jesus was not present when the New Testament was written and, thus, could not intervene editorially and prevent such bitter references from being written in scripture. Also, Jesus was not physically present to argue with future anti-Jewish interpreters. We do, however, remember that Jesus himself was no "Christian." He was a Jew. The Bible, however, has at least one voice speaking directly against such broad and biased comments as those. The apostle Paul was physically around to add his two cents' worth. In three chapters of Romans (chapters 9, 10, and 11), Paul answers the question: "What about those of the Jewish faith-tradition in light of God's revelation of faith and salvation through Jesus?" Paul's conclusion, drawn from his understanding of the scriptures, is that God made a covenant promise to the Jewish people through Abraham and Sarah—a promise fulfilled in a Jewish rabbi-healer named Jesus—and God does not go back, or renege, on God's promises. Not ever! (Remember: Grace rules!)

If God's covenant promise to those of the Jewish faith-tradition continues irrevocably, "Christ-killers" is a label of bigotry based on anger in the early Christian communities such as those to whom Matthew and John wrote. Their anger was understandably directed toward Jewish religious leaders who opposed the new Christian movement in their synagogues and in the temple. There were even accounts of persecution toward the early Christians. But to use these biases as a literal interpretation and therefore condemnation of Jews throughout history is to misuse scripture in a harmful and destructive way. It makes the Bible more about our human words than the Word of God present in the Jesus Christ of scripture.

Jesus, as Jewish rabbi and student of the scriptures, was not a literalist when interpreting scripture. More than once (we're told), Jesus introduced teachings by saying, "You have heard it said . . . But I say to you . . ." (see Matthew 5:27–28, 31–32, 33–34, 38–39, 43–44). In these cases, Jesus' interpretations of scripture are broader and are applied to more situations than the interpretations of the literalists.

Jesus also seemed to recognize that parts of scripture contradict other parts of scripture. One place in the Bible states that God punishes sinners (Proverbs 24:16). This idea is that when something bad happens, it probably was your fault because you sinned in some way. (See Job for an argument against this as well.) In Luke 13:1–5, however, Jesus challenges that interpretation "head on." Jesus interprets that "bad things" happen not as punishment on people for their sinfulness, but rather that a tragedy can happen to anyone. Further, he teaches that no one is so much an insider with God that repentance is not necessary, including repentance for thinking oneself better than others. If Jesus was not a literalist when knowing about

Proverbs 24:16 and interpreting events described in Luke 13, why should any of us think we should be literalists? Jesus is our stumbling block if we apply beliefs or interpretations to him that manipulate others or ourselves and that were not Jesus' beliefs and interpretations in the first place.

WORD OR WORDS?

Let's go back to Jamie at the sleepover with her teen friends. Jamie has heard that if someone doesn't believe one particular interpretation of the Bible, then that person is not considered Christian. We've discussed how off-base this position is. As was said, she wonders what her mother, a Presbyterian elder, believes about this and what her pastor would have to say. That's our question too: How do Presbyterians approach the Bible and the ways it guides our faith and life?

First and foremost, Presbyterians believe there is a greater purpose for scripture in "the big picture" of life, history, and God's relationship with God's people. What might that be? Or, how might that be? Scripture's greater purpose—through stories and teachings and prayers—is to reveal the past, present, and future of God's love, justice, and power in relationship with people and creation, all with a goal of life being made new. Presbyterians focus less on the literal human words and more on discerning the Word testified to in those human words. Always we strive to look beyond the black and white letters to encounter the Spirit present in the stories, prayers, and teachings of the Bible.

How does this understanding of scripture influence our approach to scripture? First, this approach recognizes much (even all) of scripture has passed down from generation to generation certain themes and ideas about God. The themes that reappear over and over are often more highly regarded because they show up repeatedly. This approach is different from one taken by many people who use proof-texting to make their assertion of truth. In proof-texting, a person cites one particular verse to support an argument. It has been said, you could proof-text any idea you can come up with. The approach we prefer takes seriously how certain themes, for example, are consistent throughout Jesus' teachings. Such themes may be regarded as having more weight in a given argument than one particular verse. We, therefore, measure "scripture against scripture" to gain a deeper and truer understanding of God's intent for us in scripture.[6]

Presbyterians (and others) believe it's important to examine scripture in Hebrew and Greek when possible and to consider differences in various English translations. We also value studying the cultures and assumptions of Bible writers in their day and time. This includes studying the nuances of language. (We saw how important that was in the last chapter.) Additionally, we strive to hear the many voices underlying any particular text. The Bible is a library of people's experiences of God shaped by their culture and context. And in our reading of that library we can encounter God ourselves. This is why we strive to listen to the Word among all the words of scripture.

One nonliteralist, noninerrantist way to approach scripture is by understanding that scripture is both a gathering of words and a testimony to and by God's Word (with a capital "W"). There's an eternal Word of God in the midst and through the words of scripture. Proverbs 8:1–21 and 8:22–9:6 characterize God's Wisdom as an eternal Word of positive teaching. John 1:1–5 and 1:14–18, as well as Colossians 1:15–20, testify to Jesus as the embodiment of God's eternal Word.

Jesus, then, with his life and ministry, helps us to understand better God's personality. Jesus further helps us to hear God's Word through the words of scripture (some of which are in contradiction to others) by encouraging study, reason, prayer, interpreted experiences, and grateful service to others as avenues through which God's eternal Word meets us in human events and relationships.

We believe God encounters us through scripture and, through these encounters, day by day changes our lives. It's also been said that our reading of the Bible as scripture is secondary to the primary ability of the Bible as scripture to "read" us.[7] As scripture "reads us" and we comprehend something of that "reading," God's life-made-new encounters us and comes alive within us. We are blessed and we are challenged as well.

Individual responses to God's Word are not always positive. Luke 4:16–30 relates the incident of Jesus reading scripture and preaching in his "home" synagogue in Nazareth. Jesus that day told stories from scripture that revealed God's graciousness to "outsiders." (Jesus was probably proud of Martin Luther King who preached a very similar message.) The religious people of the Nazareth synagogue worshiping with Jesus back then thought of those to whom Jesus referred as different from and as inferior to themselves as citizens of Nazareth.

The stories to which Jesus referred were from 1 Kings 17:1 and 17:8–16 and 2 Kings 5:1–14. The worshipers at Nazareth, as the story goes from Luke 4, became enormously angry at Jesus' method of interpreting scripture. Jesus' method sought to hear the timeless, truthful, healing Word of God through the many words of scripture. His use of the scripture from Isaiah 61:1–2 and Leviticus 25:10 referred to God as One to be celebrated for God's delivering and barrier-removing power. But there's a claim on people then and now who receive God's delivering and barrier-removing power. That claim moves us beyond a "hallelujah" in receiving this power. The claim became a challenge for all God's people: to live with others as co-celebrants because God brings barriers down! The religious people of Jesus' hometown that day were angry when Jesus told of God wanting to bring down barriers that they hoped would stay in place. Their responses back then and ours today are not always positive responses as God desires, but God does not give up on us!

WHY AND HOW WE READ THE BIBLE!

Why? Because scripture presents timeless stories, teachings, and prayers that offer guidance to people through the ages. That guidance is received as the words of scripture, by God's Spirit, communicate a living Word to encounter God's people (others and us!) and to create new life within us.

And how? Not as literalists. If Jesus was not a literalist, but one who studied, observed, taught, and healed from a radical faithfulness to God, and if we acknowledge this Jesus as the One-in-flesh who is God's Eternal Word, why would we want to be literalists? If we are literalists, there's a higher degree of likelihood we will stumble over Jesus because we are pre-ferring many literal words (sometimes contradicting one another) to the nonliteralist Word-in-flesh who Jesus is.

Instead of literalism, we try to read scripture (and experience scripture reading us) with interpretations that include consideration of: (1) issues when such scripture was first, and later, told and heard; (2) how the scrip-ture being examined has been influenced by previous scripture; (3) Jesus' teachings on similar matters; and (4) what developments in and around us are related to the particular scripture being studied. Such developments either cry out for God's holy love drawing near or give evidence positively that God's holiness is being experienced.

Reading the Bible this way takes effort—prayer, research, study, thought, conversation. But for those willing to read, pray, research, study, think, and converse with one another as participants in communities of faith, the effort will be rewarded with multiple experiences of the Bible as being full of words that testify to the Word of God giving life fully.

And what's more, those who study scripture this way will be strength-ened for life's hardest times and life's most difficult struggles because familiarity with the words of scripture will make the presence of God's Word all the more clear as God draws near (see Luke 24:13–35).

So, "Is the Bible the literal Word of God, or just a long, boring book?" It is neither. And, as God's gift, contradictions and all, it is so much more. It's the well from which God's Word is drawn for drink as we thirst for that Word in life. It is the source and sustenance of our living relationship with God. It challenges us; it comforts us; it points us to ways of life with new horizons. The Bible is God's Word to us. We should not cheapen it by trying to make it fit literally into categories for which it was not intended. If Jesus was not a literalist, why would we think Jesus wants us to be literalists?

So What Do *You* Think?

1. Have you ever experienced this debate about the Bible between fundamentalists and nonfundamentalists? What happened? What were the issues and questions?

2. Read again the story of Jamie at the beginning of this chapter. If you were in Jamie's situation, would you: (a) say something like, "Jesus was not a literalist. Why should I be one?" (b) say nothing, but think, "Jesus was not a literalist. Why should I be one?" or (c) say or think something different (and, if so, what)?

3. Have you ever had times when something in the Bible really spoke to you? If so, describe one of those times. Did the Bible comfort you? confront you? challenge you? motivate you? Did it make you feel some other way?

Are You Going to Heaven, or to Tulsa?[1]

ARE YOU SURE YOU ARE GOING TO HEAVEN?

AGNES'S ANXIETY

Agnes had a friend, a young man who had tragically committed suicide. Her grief and sadness were heightened not only by the minister at the funeral, who asked, "Are you going to heaven when you die?" but also by hearing people whisper the idea that her friend was condemned to hell for committing suicide. Agnes's friends were even more forthright in their opinion that he was probably in hell for his actions. "The Bible tells us that suicide is an unforgivable sin. I don't know why he would jeopardize his soul by killing himself," one of Agnes's friends said to her. While Agnes didn't believe that her friend who committed suicide should be divinely punished for an obvious act of desperation, she wasn't sure how to respond to this other friend's certainty about the question of heaven and hell. She wasn't even sure she believed in life after death.

The loss of her friend and her own sense of uncertainty made her wonder what kind of God would punish people for being in such pain that they would kill themselves. Agnes was worried for herself too, anxious that she didn't know for sure if she would be going to heaven or not.

The questions of heaven and hell are of primary importance for the neo-evangelical in the Bible Belt. In many ways, the concern about the destiny of one's soul in the afterlife is the motivating force for accepting Jesus into your heart. As we noted earlier, many neo-evangelicals consider the future salvation of your soul to be dependent on your conversion, your acceptance of Jesus into your heart. "If you don't, God won't save you." Therefore, the ultimate reason for accepting Jesus is to ensure your place in heaven. The life of faith is really just a kind of "heaven insurance" so that you can be certain of being fitted with wings and a halo. You "take out the policy" by believing and doing the right things, and then it's paid off when you die and you get your reward. Heaven is the place for people who paid the right dividends on their hell insurance. (we never thought of ministers as insurance salespersons, but it fits this metaphor.)

> God is a dancer with God's people, a dancer of tap, soft-shoe, tango, limbo, polka, twist, minuet, two-step, disco, ballet, and more. God gets jiggy.[2]

Obviously, there are a number of problems with this view of the world, or the afterworld. Not the least is the prevailing attitude that it's always "our people" who get into heaven and the bad guys, usually anyone who doesn't quite believe and act the way we think they should, who end up being cast into hell. Heaven becomes an exclusive country club for the beautiful people who can look down at those sinners in the ghetto of hell and feel sorry for them.[3]

There is an arrogance about this belief that one group has the inside track into heaven while those immoral people "out there" are doomed eternally. The question soon enough becomes, "Who would want to be in a heaven filled with a bunch of self-righteous people?" It would be rather boring, don't you think? (And surely heaven cannot be boring!)

Another problem with this view of heaven and hell is that life on earth becomes more concerned with the probabilities of the future than with the realities of the present. Historically, living one's life for the promise of future reward has often been a justification for passivity toward any kind of change here on earth. The message is "Be happy even if you are a slave, or poor, or persecuted because of the color of your skin. Be happy because you know you will be rewarded in heaven. Don't rock the boat. Don't argue with authority. Don't question certain beliefs. If you do, you might be jeopardizing your soul."

This is what Karl Marx meant when he wrote about religion being "the opiate of the people."[4] Religion, Marx believed, anesthetizes people in this world with the promise that they will get their reward in the next. A major flaw in this kind of belief in heaven and hell is that faith is more about rewards in the future than living the faith in the present. In other words, the neo-evangelical emphasis on heaven and hell can create a kind of spiritual navel-gazing in which the only purpose in life is to make sure "I get into heaven." It is, ultimately, a rather selfish outlook on life where I live not for others but for my own salvation. While I may want to help others into heaven, in the end, the religious life becomes more about doing the right things to get myself (at least) into heaven. In our individualistic and self-focused culture, it is no wonder this belief system finds so many adherents.

The final problem, of course, is that the God of this belief system is not the God of scripture. The God of the Old, or First, Testament (while, admittedly, sometimes appearing rather cruel in judgment and punishment) is finally the God who continues to forgive and reach out to humanity, even when people are rejecting God and God's covenant. Scripture describes God as one who forgives an adulterous wife,[5] one who comforts despairing children,[6] one who forgives over and over again.[7] The God of Jesus Christ is a God who forgives and reaches out, not in judgment but in suffering love. God is a father who pines for a lost son, a woman who celebrates finding a lost coin, and a shepherd who leaves behind ninety-nine sheep to find the one that is lost.[8] This is not a God who, in the manner that media movie critics Siskel and Ebert made famous, sits on a throne in heaven and gives a "thumbs up" or "thumbs down."

DO PRESBYTERIANS BELIEVE IN HELL?

Whenever Presbyterian ministers are asked, "What do you think heaven or hell will be like?" we often rely on our years of study and intense exploration of the Bible and theology. We rely on knowledge gained through time spent considering spiritual matters, and we reply with all our wisdom in a simple response: "Who the hell knows?"

While this may seem glib, it nevertheless expresses the truth that finally we have no details about the reality beyond this life. We have ideas and certain beliefs, but they will always fall short of the truth of what life beyond death will actually be like. We declare, with all our faith, a belief in the promise of resurrection, but we are not able to paint a definitive picture of what the resurrected life will look like. We hope you would be rather suspicious of us if we did. Presbyterians are wary of trite theological answers, or, at least, should be.

It is interesting to look at what Jesus has to say about this question. Three of the Gospels[9] tell the story about the time a religious group called the Sadducees questioned Jesus about the resurrection. In order to understand this story, we should know that the Sadducees did not believe in the resurrection. Another group, the Pharisees, did believe in life beyond death, and there was a heated debate between the two parties about this subject.

The Sadducees asked Jesus a question designed to reveal what Jesus believed about the resurrection. According to Mosaic law, when a man died leaving his wife childless, his brother was constrained to marry the woman and raise up her children. The Sadducees then presented Jesus with a puzzling situation. There were seven brothers. The first married, and finally died without children, then the second brother married the widow, and he also died without children; and then the third, and so on, and so on, until the seventh brother also died childless. (This woman is tough on husbands!) Finally the woman dies, and the Sadducees ask, "In the resurrection, therefore, whose wife will the woman be? For the seven had married her." Rather tricky of these Sadducees, don't you think?

Jesus' response is interesting not only in what he says but also in what he doesn't say. While affirming a belief in life beyond death, he argues that the reality of resurrection is not like that here on earth. "In the resurrection they neither marry nor are given in marriage." What Jesus asserts here is that the life of resurrection is not like anything here on earth. The reality is different from what we can comprehend. Jesus does not describe the reality, he does not try to give us a description of what exactly it will look or be like. He simply points out that it will be different from what we have experienced here.

"God is not a God of the dead, but a God of the living," Jesus says. God is not about death, but about life with all its beauty and possibilities. The God of life we experience here on earth is the God of life we experience beyond death. Jesus, in responding to the Sadducees, points to something that cannot be described or understood in earthly terms but only by the mystery of God who brings life where there is death. Jesus doesn't give us an explanation. He gives us assurance of life beyond death.

In the same way, Presbyterians also believe in the God of life. Presbyterians believe in the resurrection but, like Jesus, we do not have a particular description of what life beyond death would necessarily look like. While we each may have our personal opinions about the details, the more important consideration is our belief in the God of life. In other words, we don't believe in heaven as a particular kind of place. We believe (trust) in God, the God of life. Our faith is in a God who does not even let death become a barrier to God's love.[10] Heaven, then, can simply be described as being in the presence of God. It is being filled with God's love and residing in that love forever. We do not know what that will look or feel like in particular detail, but we do know that the God we experience in Jesus Christ will not let death be the final word. We can get a taste of this heaven here on earth when we live in God's love and when we share that love with others around us. Experiencing the present-day reality of being in God's presence, we catch a glimpse of the promise and joy of life eternal, even in the here-and-now of this finite and broken world. It's a far different understanding of heaven than simply a place filled with golden streets and angels playing harps.

Conversely, we could describe hell as the absence of God. Hell isn't some fiery place beyond death where sinners are punished for lax morality or wrong belief, but hell is the reality of people denying God's presence and love. (So hell could equally be an assignment into God's presence when one hates being in the presence of the God of grace!)

There are plenty of hells on earth, where people have chosen not God's love but another reality. The hell of the Holocaust was a total denial of God, an embracing of an absence of God by people who would make their cause itself a god. The hell of racism is a denial of God's presence among people who are different simply because of their skin. The hell of addiction is choosing, for momentary pleasure and very sad dependency, a god of death over the God of life. It could be said that we do not need a hell beyond death because we expertly create our own hell here on earth. Most Presbyterians believe in hell because they see it everyday on their televisions in places like Bosnia, Kosovo, Yugoslavia, the Sudan, Somalia, etc.

There is another issue related to the question of hell and evil: the issue of belief in a devil. In the Bible Belt, the devil runs a close second to Jesus on the religious top ten list. In fact, the devil sells better, considering periodic lists of best-selling books about the Antichrist and the end of the world. (We will look at this in chapter 6.)

Do Presbyterians believe in the devil? Some do and some don't. For a person to be faithful to God, one does not necessarily personally have to believe in a particular agent of evil opposed to God in the world. The reasons for this are numerous, but, essentially, too often the belief in Satan is just another excuse not to take responsibility for our own actions in the world. "The devil made me do it" is an easy way to explain away our own brokenness and our capacity for evil. If there is a devil, we only have to look in the mirror to see his or her face sometimes.

To state a disbelief in a red guy with horns and hooves doesn't mean we don't believe there is evil in the world. There is evil. You can see it in the horrific realities of our sinful world and sometimes even in the small corners of our souls. There is no need for a devil opposed to God in the world. We humans fit that role quite nicely ourselves.

Another interesting facet of Presbyterian belief on the question of life beyond death involves an interesting phrase we speak in the Apostles' Creed. Usually in most Presbyterian churches, we will affirm our faith by reciting the Apostles' Creed. We state we believe Jesus "was crucified, dead, and buried. He descended into hell. On the third day, he rose again from the dead and ascended into heaven." Does this mean that Presbyterians, in reciting this creed, are saying they believe in a literal hell "down below" or a heaven "up above"? To take this creed literally is to miss the point. (Literalism has a way of missing these things, if you haven't noticed before.)

When we speak these words, some Presbyterians may mean a belief in a particular hell and heaven, but most often we are affirming something far more important than this. In stating that Jesus descended into hell, we are making a theological statement that there is no place God will not go to bring God's love in Jesus Christ.[11] There is no place God will not travel to bring light and hope, even to the very gates of hell. The meaning of this creedal statement is not to affirm a literal belief in hell "down there," but the much more important belief that nothing can separate us from the love of God in Christ! To believe this is also to understand that the hells we create here on earth for ourselves can be and are challenged by God. Even in such a hellhole as Auschwitz, we hear stories of faith and courage that attest to the presence of God where others would deny God's love.[12] What we are stating when we affirm the faith that "Jesus descended into hell" is a theological belief that there is no place in heaven or hell where God will not seek us out and save us. Thank God for that!

GUILT OR GRATITUDE?

We believe in grace. (Are you sick of that word yet?) This belief shapes our understanding that we live out of gratitude rather than guilt. To worry constantly if one is getting into heaven or ending up in hell is to live a life either motivated by or preoccupied with guilt, guilt over wrongs we've done to ourselves and to those around us. Have I done the right things or believed in the right things to earn my way into heaven? These kinds of questions may haunt us, guilt over our failures and human feebleness may obsess us, because we worry that our failure in matters of morality may hinder our entrance into heaven. Shame and despair are too easily the result of this kind of fear. And shame and fear hinder love more than anything else in the world. God's judgment becomes the overriding theme as we envision ourselves standing before the throne of heaven to be judged according to our deeds. Life becomes a kind of test during which any wrong move could get you tossed into the fiery lake of hell. This is a frightening way to live.

We understand that life is a gift (grace!) and that God's love comes not because we "earned points" or made the right decisions in order to get our reward later on when we die. Life is lived out of gratitude and not guilt, shaped by love and not judgment. We live a holy life not because we want to be sure we get to the "right place" after we die, but because we have experienced God's grace and wish to celebrate that gift each and every day. We live out of this sense of thankfulness and appreciation for all God has done and will do for us. The basis of life, then, is not shame but celebration; we do not live in fear but in freedom.

One interesting thing to notice in scripture is that often the first words out of the mouth of God and God's messengers when they encounter human beings is, "Do not be afraid."[13] This is important because so much human behavior is driven by fear; and when fear is the motivator, life is diminished. In fact, it's been argued that the opposite of love is not hate but fear. There cannot be compassion for another when you are afraid of that person; there cannot be mercy for the stranger when the stranger evokes fear. At the root of most of our inhumanity to each other, for example, racism and anti-Semitism, is a basic fear of the unknown. So how can fear be the motivating force for our love of God? How can guilt and fear be at the heart of our relationship with the Source of life and love?

We Presbyterians don't believe that this can happen with any significant degree of health. We take seriously God's commandment not to be afraid. What motivates our behavior is a sense of gratitude for God's gift of love. God has been so giving and welcoming, we must respond out of thanksgiving.

Our communities are characterized, then, as places of gratitude rather than guilt, of hope rather than fear. Paul beautifully states, in his letter to the church in Thessalonica, "Rejoice always, pray without ceasing, give thanks in all circumstances; for this is the will of God in Christ Jesus for you."[14] Reformed and Presbyterian churches have, for centuries, stated that the "chief end of [every human being] is to glorify God, and to enjoy [God] forever."[15] Another, more recent statement of belief also puts it beautifully: "In gratitude to God, empowered by the Spirit, we strive to serve Christ in our daily tasks and to live holy and joyful lives. . . ."[16] Our purpose then is to rejoice, enjoy, and live joyful lives in response to the gift of God's love and compassion. Life is more a celebration than a test to see the fitness of our souls.

A convincing argument can be made saying that, when we meet God in the afterlife, God's first question may well be "Why didn't you have more joy?"

One final story before we "get the hell out of here." This is a story about how Alex's mother joined the Presbyterian Church. She was living in Omaha, Nebraska, and pregnant with him when, one day, a Presbyterian minister knocked on her front door. She invited him in, and he began to tell her that they were starting up a new Presbyterian church just down the road. He wanted to invite her to attend their worship service. Having been raised in the Southern Baptist Church, she had a few questions about what Presbyterians believe. She said, "Well, my husband smokes, and, while I wish he wouldn't, I don't think he is going to hell for that."

The Presbyterian minister said, "Presbyterians believe that is between you and God, and that it is no one else's business. There are some Presbyterians who smoke, and there are some who don't."

Mom wasn't quite satisfied, and so she asked again, "Now, I like to have a drink now and again, and I don't think that is sinful either."

The minister said, "Well, some Presbyterians drink, and some don't."

Finally, Mom said, "And I really love to dance and don't see anything wrong with that either."

The minister replied, "Ma'am, all Presbyterians dance!" The next week she joined the Presbyterian Church.

We dance because we are grateful! Amen!

So What Do *You* Think?

1. What do you think Jesus could have meant when he said, "God is not a God of the dead, but a God of the living" (Matthew 22:32)?

2. Compare your views of "heaven" and "hell" now with what you thought when you were younger. Have your thoughts and beliefs changed some over the years?

3. Think about these two images as they describe the way some people live: "stewing in guilt" and "dancing in gratitude." Describe what comes to mind about these two ways of living.

Is Jesus "Lord," or Just a Good Guy?

It's hard to live as Jesus did.

Allison and Seth are next-door neighbors. Both are fifteen years old, and neither is from a family that regularly participates in the life of a community of faith. One evening, ten days before Easter, Seth is at Allison's checking on a chemistry class assignment he'd missed because of an appointment at the doctor.

The television is on, and while taking a break from molecular reconfigurations during chemical changes, they notice a commercial being broadcast for an upcoming Easter drama at a large church in a nearby city. First, there's a ten-second preview of Jesus carrying his cross through the crowds, collapsing along the way, then a ten-second scene of the crucifixion, which leads to a fifteen-second scene from the burial garden early on Sunday morning. As the name of the church and a schedule of the pageant's performances are printed along the bottom of the screen, Allison said, "That looked a little weird to me."

"What's that?" asked Seth.

"Jesus and those followers giving 'high-fives' to celebrate his being raised from the dead."

"Guess I hadn't thought about it," replied Seth, "but now that you mention it. . . ."

"From what I know," Allison said, "Jesus must have been a good guy, but what's a thinking person supposed to make of a scene outside a tomb, with the guy who was buried suddenly 'up and out' in a victory celebration with his friends, all after his life had ended and he'd been closed in there a couple of days before?"

"Maybe he wasn't completely dead when they buried him," Seth suggested.

"Possibly," Allison said, "but the narrator's voice said, 'He died for your sins. Won't you come celebrate with us the new life you too can have in a personal relationship with him? He wants to be Lord and Savior of your life.' I don't know much about the Jesus and Easter stuff, but 'high-fives' outside the grave is not really a turn-on to me."

"We could ask Charlene what she thinks. She's a member at the Episcopal Church," Seth proposed.

"Or Billy. He's a member at Southside Assembly of God," countered Allison.

"Let's call 'em, and see what they say."

"Maybe," said Allison, "but only after we finish going over your chemistry."

"Deal," agreed Seth as he turned back to the next set of review questions.

DO YOU HAVE A PERSONAL RELATIONSHIP WITH JESUS CHRIST?

Allison and Seth rightly wonder, "Who is Jesus? Who is this Jesus who was crucified, buried, and said to be alive again beyond the grave? Who is this Jesus that some call 'Lord and Savior'? Who is this Jesus with whom, it is said, we can have some sort of relationship?"

Indeed, a question Presbyterians are often asked is: Do you have a personal relationship with Jesus Christ? That is, to put it mildly, a loaded question—loaded with meanings. To begin with, the question not only implies that the questioner thinks that such a relationship with Jesus Christ is good and desirable but also carries the presumption that such a relationship is necessary for salvation. (As was noted in chapter 1: "For the neo-evangelical Christian . . . , the significant event in a Christian's salvation is this moment of acceptance or conversion.")

To get right to the point, a Presbyterian can confidently answer, "Yes, I do have a personal relationship with Jesus Christ," but more needs to be said about what Presbyterians understand by such a statement. There are three key elements involved here: Jesus, Christ, and personal relationship. Let's look at them one at a time.

Jesus—This is a name, of course, and it refers to a person who lived in history. As Allison and Seth watched the television advertisement for the upcoming Easter drama, they remarked that they didn't know much about this Jesus. What more could they know? Based on information we glean mostly from scripture and from related first-century writings, we know that Jesus was a Jewish teacher and healer, born about two thousand years ago, growing up in the area of Galilee, who, at about the age of thirty years, was crucified in Jerusalem by Roman authorities.

Christ—The word "Christ" is not a name, but a theological label. It comes from a Greek word meaning "promised" or "anointed." The same term in Hebrew is "messiah." In the First (or Old) Testament, the term "Christ" (messiah) was used to describe the hope that God would send a specially appointed person (an "anointed one") who would save God's people from their enemies and establish God's will on earth. In the Gospel of Matthew, when Peter says to Jesus, "You are the Messiah, the Son of the living God . . ." (16:16), Matthew wants us to understand that Peter is confessing his faith that this Jesus is, indeed, the *Christ*, God's promised messiah.

Although Peter may in fact have called Jesus "the Christ," just as Matthew writes, many Bible scholars hold the opinion that the term "Christ" was applied to Jesus only after the resurrection. Without question, the Gospel accounts proclaim that Jesus is the Christ, that Jesus, who suffered and died unjustly, was raised beyond death by God's power, and is the promised one of God, the fulfillment of God's covenant promise with Israel dating back to Abram and Sarai (Genesis 12). But it is likely that the church did not understand all this about Jesus until after his death and resurrection, after they were able to view him through the lens of their faith in his risen presence with them.

So when Matthew says that Peter called Jesus "the Christ" before his resurrection, this is likely a reading back into the story of Jesus' life a view of him that developed later. It is Matthew's way of saying that what we now know to be true about Jesus *because* of the resurrection—that he is the Christ—was true about him *before* the resurrection, even if Peter did not use the exact term. "If they didn't call Jesus 'Christ,'" Matthew seems to be saying, "they could have. And if they'd thought about it, they would have."[1]

So we have Jesus, and we have Christ—"Jesus Christ." Is this a name? Not exactly. It is a name and a title—Jesus (name) who is the Christ (title). The title Christ is attached to the person's name Jesus (The name "Jesus," incidentally, means "deliverer" and is a derivative of the Hebrew name Joshua).[2] As for the existence of the person Jesus, this is a matter of historical record. You don't have to be a person of faith to say that there was a

Jesus any more than you have to be a scientist to say that there was a man named Einstein—it's a historical fact. However, to say "Jesus Christ," to call this man Jesus "the Christ," is to combine the name of a particular historical person with the mystery of what is claimed in faith. Remember that combination: history, mystery, and faith.

Personal Relationship—Now we are ready to think about what it could mean to have a "personal relationship" with Jesus the Christ. To say that we have a personal relationship with Jesus the Christ is another way of saying that the man Jesus in his role as the Christ makes a difference to us here and now. Do Presbyterians believe Jesus makes a difference? Yes. Absolutely. But how?

When Presbyterians talk about the difference that Jesus Christ makes, they often use two terms: the "person" and the "work" of Jesus Christ. The "person" of Jesus Christ refers to the belief that Jesus Christ makes a difference particularly because of *who* he is—his identity. Jesus was connected to God in a way that is unique. Historically, the church has argued over and wrestled with how to describe this uniqueness, saying such things as Jesus Christ was an equal person in the Trinity or that he was fully human while at the same time being fully divine.[3]

The "work" of Jesus Christ refers to *what he did*, or the accomplishment that theologically is called "atonement." Atonement means the "making as one again" what had become broken, alienated, and estranged. We, of course, as sinful human beings, are broken, alienated, and estranged. Presbyterians join with other Christians in saying that God did not abandon sinful humanity, staying aloof in heaven, but that in Jesus, God became personally involved in repairing broken human beings. In Jesus Christ, the holy God became "God is with us" (Matthew 1:23c, quoting Isaiah 7:14; 8:8, 10).[4]

But how did God do this? How did Jesus Christ accomplish the "work" of atonement? Over the years, at least three different general interpretations of atonement have been described and argued. Presbyterians have found meaning and value in all three:

1. *"Christus Victor" (Christ the Victor)*—This view sees Jesus Christ as doing battle with the powers of sin and evil and defeating them. Jesus is a kind of military hero in the war to save humanity—but unlike ordinary military heroes, Jesus lived a life of gentleness and compassion and he surrendered to death on a cross. On Easter, by God's power Jesus was raised to new life and granted the victory that liberates humanity from the evil powers.

2. *Substitution*—This view sees Jesus on the cross as taking our place, substituting himself for us and taking on himself that anger of God and the punishment that is rightfully deserved by all of us as sinners.

3. *Moral Influence*—This view sees what Jesus did on the cross as a powerful expression of God's love for humanity. This extraordinary example leads and moves God's people to repentance and the experience of reconciliation.[5]

Put this all together, then, and we can begin to understand what Presbyterians mean by a "personal relationship with Jesus Christ." They mean that a man who lived two thousand years ago—Jesus—was no ordinary man. He was also the Christ, God's anointed one, sent to save sinful humanity. Because of who he was and what he did, Jesus made atonement for our sin, repairing the broken relationship between humanity and God. This Jesus Christ was raised by God from the dead and lives today, working in our lives to liberate us from all that would destroy us.

For Presbyterians past and present, a personal relationship with Jesus who is the Christ makes a difference in life and history. How that relationship is experienced, interpreted, and understood, throughout the years of a person's life, may vary from childhood through adulthood. It's always, however, a process of studying, discussing, praying, and considering. Remember the combination of history, mystery, and faith!

You and we and all who consider Jesus and God's call through Word and Spirit are part of the process of history, mystery, and faith. Interpretations and affirmations about Jesus may change from childhood through adulthood. That is natural. In fact, it could be classified a matter of sadness, even tragedy, if any of us ever stopped considering and reconsidering God, Jesus, Spirit, God's people, and the relationship of these.

Never, though, is the personal relationship with God through Jesus (as important as that is) all that's involved between God and God's people.

PERSONAL SALVATION AND/OR COMMUNITY CELEBRATION?

Remember the story of Allison and Seth at the beginning of this chapter? Neither of them thought they knew too much about Jesus. Even so, something made them resistant to the idea that the risen Jesus would give "high-fives" to his disciples on Easter. Allison and Seth rightly sense that something is off-balance or amiss in the television commercial they saw about the upcoming Easter pageant.

Indeed, according to scripture (see Matthew 28; Luke 24; John 20 and 21; and Acts 1), the resurrection of Jesus provokes as much fear, anxiety, puzzlement, amazement, and questioning, as it does joy. This is true among those who actually encounter the risen Christ as well as among those who just hear about it from others. If Easter were only about personal salvation—me and Jesus—then only joyful "high-fives" outside the empty tomb would make sense. But Easter goes way beyond just personal salvation, and this is why it creates both joy and fear, amazement and anxiety. Because of Easter, the world can never be the same again. We can never be the same. The God who sent Jesus into the world, sends us into the world, too, to do God's work. Because of Easter, the whole world is ultimately involved, and Jesus' disciples are challenged to learn that God's call and life for them include others, all others, whether those others actually confess the same faith in Jesus or not. All are neighbors; all are brothers and sisters under the Lordship of God in Jesus.

This is why Christian faith is lived out in something called "church." The word "church" means those "called out," or "called together from out of a larger group." God's people in Jesus are called out together for service as we celebrate and share with others the new life God gives. This faith asks more of us than simply either celebrating in joy or being stuck in our anxiety, puzzlement, amazement, and questioning. Beyond any of our very human reactions, we learn and are led to realize that "Christian hope is not limited to the fulfillment of individual life. [Christian hope] insists that personal and communal hope are inseparable."[6]

This understanding has also been argued by John Calvin, the mid-sixteenth-century theologian whose thought has been so formative for Presbyterians. Calvin wrote:

> We ought to embrace the whole human race without exception in a single feeling of love; here there is no distinction between barbarian and Greek, worthy and unworthy, friend and enemy, since all should be contemplated in God, not in themselves. . . . Therefore, if we rightly direct our love, we must first turn our eyes not to man, the sight of whom would more often engender hate than love, but to God, who bids us extend to all men the love we bear to [God], that this may be an unchanging principle: whatever the character of the man, we must yet love him because we love God.[7]

Jesus' person and work have roots in history. Jesus' person and work also are surrounded by the mystery of God through the faith claim of the disciples and the church that Jesus is Messiah (Christ). And the mystery of God is continually involved in the shaping of human lives as Jesus lived and taught, that by God's grace all human beings belong to God and are created, redeemed, and given new life from birth through death as members of the human family.

If Allison and Seth called a Presbyterian friend to ask about Jesus, they might hear something like "Presbyterians believe that Jesus is Lord, but each person, day by day, year by year, as a disciple, is called to study and consider prayerfully how Jesus' life and Lordship have a shaping effect on each one's life."

Presbyterian pastor Bob Walkup, it is said, once preached a memorable sermon in which the refrain was something like "It's hard to be a Christian!" Yes, it is hard to be a Christian, especially in the sense that it's hard to live as Jesus did. It's hard to live as Jesus urged disciples to live: loving those who are different from oneself and one's group; learning from those who are different from oneself and one's group.

It's hard to be a Christian, but that's what we're attempting when we both join with others in celebrating God's new life for the world and join with others for serving as God leads us among God's wonderfully diverse people.

So What Do *You* Think?

1. Using whatever means you choose—creative writing, mime, music, art—depict your relationship to Jesus.

2. Suppose you got the chance to interview Jesus about his life and work. What are the most important questions you would like to ask? How do you think Jesus would answer those questions, and why?

Are Only 144,000 Saved?

WHAT ARE THE ODDS?

Julia and Joe leaned against the front grill and bumper of her car on the large parking lot of a grocery store. It was 10:20 on a Friday night, and Julia's friend, Danielle, had gone with Joe's friend, Tom, for a cruise down the avenue in the train of forty other cars driven by their high school peers. When Joe looked across four lanes of traffic, he noticed the marquee at the church across the street: Sunday's Message: "Will You Be Among the Saved?"

"I wonder what the preacher will say about that on Sunday morning?" he wondered aloud.

"Are you interested enough to go?" Julia asked.

"I don't think so," he replied, "but it's an interesting question."

"Yeah," Julia said, "maybe it has more angles to it than even the preacher thinks."

"How do you mean?" inquired Joe.

"My grandmother once told me that in the book of Revelation somewhere it says that the number of those saved will be 144,000. I figure that's two good-sized college or pro football stadiums' worth. And, if you only take the two thousand years since Jesus, that's an average of seventy-two people per year, not to mention the fact that the average will be decreasing for every year that time goes on."

"Hmmm . . ." murmured Joe. "Worldwide that's not very many."

"Not too many," said Julia.

"Think about a million people sometimes turning out to see the Pope when he travels out to visit different countries," Joe suggested.

"Less than one out of five, and that's if no one else from any other century is saved," Julia wryly noted.

"Just think," Joe calculated. "If that preacher takes Revelation literally, maybe no one he'll be preaching to on Sunday will be saved in the end."

"Odds are," Julia responded. "Hey! That Toyota almost hit that Honda!"

When Julia's grandmother said that the book of Revelation says somewhere that the number of those saved will be 144,000, she was referring to Revelation 14:1–5. We'll specifically consider the book of Revelation in the next chapter, but Julia and Joe (and the preacher of the sermon advertised on the marquee), whether they were aware of it or not, were considering what theologians call the "inner workings" of God as God goes about the processes of creating and accomplishing salvation.

Looking at the "inner workings" of God is tricky business. After all, "who has known the mind of the Lord?"[1] But let's be bold and try "to go there." Let's do so, though, aware of the difficulty and conscious of the limits in such an effort.

DO YOU BELIEVE IN PREDESTINATION?

The church marquee Julia and Joe saw read "Will You Be Among the Saved?" This could imply that there is a fixed, predetermined number of "the saved." Julia's grandmother had heard that the Bible fixed the number of the saved at 144,000.

Do Presbyterians believe in a fixed, predetermined group of "the saved"? Sometimes people say, yes, Presbyterians do believe this because they believe in "predestination." Well, do Presbyterians believe in predestination? The short answer is that Presbyterians don't *believe in* predestination; they *believe only in* God. The longer answer is more complex, though, because Presbyterians believe God always knows more than we can know.

At the heart of Reformed and Presbyterian faith-tradition is the understanding that God is always greater than we can ever imagine. (Some would use the word "sovereign" to describe this greater-than-creation aspect of God.) God, then, is the One who has "the first word and the last word" (Genesis 1:3 and Revelation 1:8) and who is present for all the words and actions, all the developments and lives in between.

Therefore predestination is not a notion that anyone needs to avoid, as if accused of witchcraft or polygamy or illicit sex. We do need to say that predestination is not a definite answer to a question like, How does God know who's saved? Predestination is, rather, one explanation of God in God's relational greatness that does not ignore God's great gift of human freedom.

God is a great surgeon.

Presbyterian-types believe that God has given humanity the tremendous gift of freedom. It simply would be a mistake, though, to argue that human beings are "absolutely free 'moral agents'" as some groups in the church (such as extreme Pelagians and Arminians) have wanted to argue across the centuries.[2] This somewhat philosophical interpretation historically has differentiated Presbyterians from our Baptist (and, later, our Methodist) cousins more than any other element of the faith we share (though there are more such "sovereignty-of-God-inclinations" among some Baptist-types than others).

Predestination does not mean that God has preprogrammed every action or that God necessarily even knows or has a purpose ahead of time for every development and action. (Although it is often said, especially in the aftermath of a horrific occurrence: "Everything happens for some purpose God has in mind." What mindless phrases we say when no words would be better than the words we end up saying! Remember Luke 13:1–5 mentioned in chapter 2.)

If God knows "the first and the last," God may well have decided to allow circumstances and genetics and randomness to constitute and play a major role in the universe. God may even have decided to set certain boundaries on God's own involvement in creation or with people. God may have chosen never to "manipulate" circumstances or may have chosen to become involved in circumstances only in a limited fashion. Or just the opposite: God may, when God chooses, always manipulate situations and circumstances.

In what ways has God chosen and does God choose to be involved with God's people? These are open-ended questions, the answers to which lie "in the mind of the Lord" only. According to the biblical witness, though, it's unmistakable that God is capable of knowing "the first word and the last word"; and God is insistent on drawing near to God's people in judgment and with mercy, all for the health and the wholeness of those people.

A next question might well be:

DO PRESBYTERIANS BELIEVE THAT SOME ARE SAVED AND SOME ARE DAMNED?

This question is similar to the question asked in chapter 2, "Do Presbyterians believe the Bible is the literal word of God?" Much like what was said in response to that question, Presbyterians through the centuries have believed differently from one another on the question of "some being saved and some being damned."

In the 1500s, the theologian John Calvin, gathering clues particularly from certain New Testament passages (such as Romans 8:28–38 and Ephesians 1:3–14), argued that God had chosen some people to be saved (the phrase used then was "elected some to salvation").[3] These people who had been chosen for salvation were called to live out that salvation as witnesses to God's glory in their earthly lives. This is the original meaning of "predestination," that some have been chosen by God from the beginning to live as witnesses to God's saving power. Because the emphasis of this view falls on one side of the equation—on salvation and those who are chosen to be saved—this is sometimes called "single predestination."

But, if some people are chosen for salvation, does it not logically follow that some other people are chosen *not* to be saved? Calvin, and especially students of Calvin who lived after him, began to develop this two-sided logic: God has chosen some for salvation, and others (logically speaking) God has damned.[4] Because this deals with both the "saved" and the "damned," this is called "double predestination," and a key Presbyterian creedal statement, the Westminster Confession of 1647 (a hundred years after Calvin, and from England rather than Calvin's Switzerland), affirms this theological perspective (some "saved" and others "unable to be saved") as the wisdom and will of God.[5]

However, not all Presbyterians have rested easy with either the single or the double predestination ideas. In 1903, the Presbyterian Church of the

United States of America wrestled with this whole business of predestination, finally arriving at something like a modified "single predestination" affirmation.[6] Even though this affirmation claims that it is God who saves and it is God who chooses those who are saved, it also leaves room for human freedom and decision-making in the "living out" of that election. This more flexible and free interpretation allows for a greater emphasis on the Holy Spirit, mission outreach, and evangelism as crucial parts of the church's ministry in Jesus' name.

In recent years, more and more people—including possibly a large number of Presbyterians—have expressed a view of salvation that can be called "biblical universalism." "Biblical universalism" is distinct from "relativistic universalism," which says "everybody is saved because everybody is okay as a human being." "Biblical universalism" says, rather, that all fall short of God's intentions and are sinners (Romans 3:23). Everyone is, in fact, damned by the nature of being human and the way each lives out that humanity in sinful and destructive ways (more about this in chapter 8 on "sin" and "repentance"). The "flip side of that coin" is that God's saving activity in covenant with Israel and known in Jesus has an extremely far-reaching (even "universal"!) effect. This could be so far-reaching that, in the mystery of God's love, which cannot be earned, all will be saved because that is God's will!

Literalists, of course, argue, "What then do we make of biblical references to the 'fires of hell' (Matthew 5:22; 7:19; 18:8; 25:41; Revelation 29:14)?" We've already noted that literal interpretations of many scriptures are problematic. However, we've also recognized that there are parts of everyone's character that we prefer not to have illuminated by the mind and character of God, before whom (the prayers of the church tell us) "no secrets are hid" (paraphrasing Psalm 44:21).

Speaking of the secrets of our character and this debate of "saved to heaven" and "damned to hell," there are attitudes within us that God can diagnose long before we have a clue. Put another way, some of our attitudes and their consequences are secrets to us, even though God fully knows how we stand (or fall!) in those matters.

A Presbyterian minister by the name of John Danhof was visiting a church as a guest lecturer. During a question-and-response time following the lecture, a member of the congregation puzzled over whatever Danhof had suggested. "Dr. Danhof," the man said, "if I sit down at the banquet table in heaven and have, sitting across from me, someone with whom I strongly disagree politically and have, sitting to my left and right, people I never wanted to live next to on earth, I don't think I'm going to like that very much."

"You could be right," Dr. Danhof responded. "That could just be hell for you!"

Are we saying here, then, that there is no literal hell or literal heaven? We are saying that if one means that a literal hell and literal heaven have a literal location on the map of the universe, then, yes, there is no such spatial location either for punishment or reward. We are not saying without a doubt that there is no spiritual hell or heaven, but that there are at least unanswerable questions about how these realities exist.

Many Presbyterians, in good conscience, believe it's helpful to speak of God's judgment and mercy as two sides of the same saving sword (or scalpel!) in God's relating to God's people (Isaiah 49:2; Hebrews 4:12; Revelation 1:16; 2:12,16; 19:15). All "fall under" the surgery of God who is "operating" on us all through life (and beyond?!) with the gracious "scalpel" of judgment and mercy.

Of course, this is a matter of faith. You can't prove God is this way, nor can anyone else; yet "biblical universalism" takes God's saving nature and people's sinful nature with absolute seriousness, including the notion that our personal decisions (even our decisions "accepting Jesus Christ as Lord and Savior") do not and cannot save us.

ELECTED TO WHAT?

If, then, God mysteriously and graciously elects or chooses us for salvation because God loves us so much and is so passionately willing to seek us out in life with that salvation, we may well ask, what are we elected to?

Moving away from the heaven and hell afterlife categories, most Presbyterian-types would concede that there's plenty of hell to worry about and, we hope, plenty of heaven to celebrate in the earthly here and now.

The Presbyterian Church (U.S.A.) *Book of Order* states that God elects God's people both "for service and for salvation,"[7] which means that God freely chooses God's people both (1) so they may receive grace in life for healing and wholeness and (2) so they will serve God among God's people, this for upbuilding the larger community which is God's world.

In spite of the givenness of human limitations and sin in areas such as ability, emotion, character, actions, and relationships, there is apparently no place God is unwilling to go in order to comfort, strengthen, encourage, and save God's people.[8] If there is no place God will not go to save God's people, surely there's no place God will not accompany God's people who are serving others as God calls them to serve.

Yet there's a distinction we need clearly to make. It's between serving others and living with an agenda for others. Living with an agenda for others is self-motivated and self-serving. Serving as the Lord of heaven and earth calls us to serve demonstrates an openness that is not manipulative but rather leads each one to be available for serving others respectfully and for serving with others respectfully. We're called to serve in this way, realizing that such others may, or may never, recognize God's grace blessing in whatever ways God's grace does bless them. Such others may, or may never, respond publicly to God with gratitude. Such others may, or may never, change their lives to be "more Christian" in our judgment. Such others may, or may never, culturally be "as we are" or in agreement with us on matters of faith and practice.

And if God is truly sovereign, it also can be said that God works where there is no naming of God's name, that God works among those who don't "know God" as we have experienced God, and that God works where we believers do not perceive or understand God to be working. This understanding of God who is truly sovereign allows God to be truly God on God's terms, not according to our understanding of God. It does not take away our freedom of choice in life-decisions, nor does it take away the component of human choice from the complex makeup of the universe. This understanding does deny that we humans ever have the power to "save" ourselves with our own choices.

WHY WE SERVE IN GOD'S WORLD!

For Presbyterians, even before there was such a name, some of God's people have understood themselves as called to honor a God who . . .

- knew them before they knew God;
- is known through the revelations of God's self, particularly through Israel and in Jesus, but who still remains mysterious and at the deepest level incomprehensible;
- goes anywhere for the health and salvation of God's people; and
- is passionately "for" human beings with the destiny of their salvation and wholeness ever in mind, even when having that destiny in mind can only be thought of as a "pre-destiny" or "predestination"!

Julia and Joe are on target to think it is rather limiting for God to save only 144,000 people. The question for Joe and Julia and each one of the rest of us is more than a speculative question of whether God knows ahead of time about our salvation or not, or whether our salvation depends on our choice exercised decisively at one definable moment or not. The question of importance for all of us every day is, How will we honor the God who has created life as holy, as worth redeeming, and as worth loving from its best moments to its worst?

Even if Joe and Julia choose not to be excited about the preaching or the biblical interpretation at the church across the street from the grocery store parking lot, Presbyterians would hope they become excited about serving God who knows them and passionately desires their discipleship. For God also knows their destiny as people of God to be healed and made whole in and by God's grace.

So What Do *You* Think?

1. Can you remember a time when you clearly and definitely thought that God directly caused something to happen—like a change in the weather, a recovery from illness, or a history teacher *not* giving a pop quiz? Do you still believe as you did at that time? Why? Or why not?

2. If you were God and you knew how much trouble and suffering are in the world, would you intervene to stop all the pain? Why? Or why not?

3. If we are too certain about our "rightness" (or righteousness) in God's eyes, we may presume we know what's best for others. Can you think of a time when someone "meant well" in trying to do something for you, but as the situation turned out, you did not appreciate what was done?

When Will the World End, or Did It End in the 1960s?

WHERE WILL YOU BE WHEN THE RAPTURE OCCURS?

SAM AND THE BUMPER STICKER

Sam was driving down the road when he saw a bumper sticker on the car in front of him: "Warning: When the Rapture Occurs, This Car Will Be Driverless." He wasn't quite sure what it meant. When he asked his dad later on that day, his dad just shook his head and said something about the end of the world some kooky religious people believe will happen soon. This only confused Sam more. So when he visited with some friends he had heard say something about the end of the world, they were surprised he wasn't ready for the end times. "Don't you know the world is coming to a fiery end soon? Aren't you ready for Jesus to come back and punish the sinners of the world and those opposed to God who are aligned with the Antichrist? Don't you know if you will be taken up in the rapture to be with God into God's glorious kingdom?"

Sam wasn't sure how to respond to their questions. His youth group had never talked about the subject, and when he had asked his youth leader if they could read Revelation, she got a panicked look in her eye and said defensively, "I think we will study that book when Jesus returns, so he can explain it to us." Sam was even more confused than ever.

Questions about the end of the world, the rapture, and the Antichrist are particularly perplexing for youth and adults as we begin a new millennium. Predictions of cataclysms, prophecies of doom, and suicidal cults are in the news, and interest in questions about the end of the world has grown as more and more people appear to be fascinated with whether the Messiah will return in all "his" glory sooner rather than later.[1]

One of the largest selling books of the 1970s was *The Late Great Planet Earth*,[2] in which the author predicted that the end of the world was imminent. The popularity of the book and author have not diminished, even though his predictions have proven false on a number of occasions. Recently, a fictionalized account of the end of the world according to Revelation has risen to the best-seller lists, even in the secular world.[3] Predictions and, some might say, panic about the possibility of the end of the world are coming to the fore as more and more people ponder the future.

It is helpful to realize that this is not a new phenomenon. People have been talking, questioning, predicting the end of the world since the days before Jesus was born. A group of Jews called the Essenes were so sure the end of the world was imminent that they went off and formed their own communes preparing for the end.[4] Around the time of Jesus' birth, various folk attempted to identify one person or another as the messiah, who would bring the Roman Empire to an end and begin a new era for the nation of Israel.[5] Even Jesus' disciples thought that he was going to bring in God's kingdom while he was still alive, and they were quite confused when he ended up dead on a cross. The early church's experience with the resurrected Lord often resulted in belief that God's kingdom was just around the corner and that they would see God's new world before they died.[6] Paul even recommends to the early church members that they not get married because Jesus' imminent return would make marriage unnecessary.[7]

The history of the church is filled with stories of sects and cults that thought Jesus' return was near. Although the degree of intensity about these end-time expectations has varied from one group to another,[8] what all these groups have in common is one truth. **They were all wrong!**

The theology of the neo-evangelical churches is often concerned with the question of the end times. Among them, Revelation can be among the most quoted of the Bible's books, and a great motivation for converting people stems from the urgency of the coming end of the world. There are even preachers who constantly analyze modern historical events in an attempt to relate such events to certain references in Revelation.[9] Often, but not always, the Antichrist is associated with an enemy of the United States (interesting!).[10] Another funny coincidence is that Jesus, when he returns, is imagined to be a blue-eyed man of European ancestry. (We have always fantasized that Jesus' return wouldn't be like anything we would expect because when he came the first time, it was as a poor Jewish carpenter's son rather than as a king. We have a notion that Jesus will look less like Charlton Heston and more like Whoopie Goldberg when he/she comes back!) Whatever the details, neo-evangelicals often spend great energy espousing and preaching preparation for the end of the world.

Before we go further with this subject, it is important that we understand the many terms and phrases that shape conversation about this subject. Based on a "literal" interpretation (we know that is impossible!) of the book of Revelation, many neo-evangelical Christians believe that there will be a certain period when a list of "events of the end time" will occur. This historical period will be characterized by earthquakes, famine, and war.[11] At some point, there will occur an event called "the rapture," during which the faithful will be caught up into heaven[12] to avoid any further pain on the earth. This is described as a beautiful and magical moment in which those who have been truly part of the church are lifted up bodily to their reward in heaven with God. But woe to those left behind! They have one chance to get themselves straightened out, for this is the time of tribulation, when the Antichrist and his forces take over the world. You can recognize who is part of the Antichrist's army by a mark: the number 666.[13] The Antichrist is an evil force, usually a person aligned against God and Jesus, who enjoys some success on earth ruling the world. But then Jesus comes with a cavalry of angels to enlist those who have found faith. A great battle called Armageddon ensues between Christ and the Antichrist.[14] Jesus wins, and there is a great kingdom of joy and peace all over the world. It's a rather bloody vision, but "the good guys live happily ever after."

Once again we perceive that the emphasis for the neo-evangelical tradition is on one's preparation and one's actions in the saving of one's soul. And once again we see that fear can be a major motivating factor for converting to Christ. If you are not one with Christ, then you could be left behind during the rapture. And for those poor souls left behind, there is much suffering and war to endure before one is deemed worthy to be taken up into heaven. Life on earth in the apocalypse is not pretty, and it is not for the weak.

That's part of the problem with this vision of the end of the world. God is a God of wrathful punishment, who looks more like General Patton than Jesus Christ. God's actions seem more appropriate for a military war than the movement of a God of love. And what do we do with all Jesus' words speaking of a kingdom of grace and forgiveness? How can we reconcile the God of Jesus Christ with God, as God is simplistically interpreted, in the Revelation to John?

DO PRESBYTERIANS BELIEVE IN THE BOOK OF REVELATION?

Before we tackle this question, it is important to underscore why Presbyterians do not follow the practice of identifying a day or time when God's kingdom will arrive. The reason is biblical. Jesus wouldn't and couldn't say when this time would be. We're told that he expressly stated, "about that day and hour no one knows, neither the angels of heaven, nor the Son, but only the Father."[15] It is also stated in Acts that, following Jesus' resurrection, some of his disciples asked a question to which he responded emphatically, "It is not for you to know the times or periods that the Father has set by his own authority."[16] Why is it that those who claim a biblical knowledge of when and where the end of the world will occur seem to deemphasize these passages of scripture, to the degree that they seem nonexistent? How can anyone ever claim such knowledge when scripture states in no uncertain terms that no one will know when it will happen?

Presbyterians are, therefore, convinced that questions about the particulars of day and time for the end of the world are not any of our business. We seek to live our lives trusting in God's grace and reminding ourselves that whatever happens in terms of God's future for God's world will be taken care of in God's sufficiency and grace. It's important not to be preoccupied with the future but focused on this present moment. Jesus desires that we be awake to this day and time and, therefore, open to what God is doing right now. God is present in this moment acting to save the world, not just in the future. Because we trust that God is sovereign and will still be a loving and saving God in the future, we are free from a paralyzing fear of the future, free to seek God's kingdom in the present.

We would argue that a Presbyterian understanding of the book of Revelation is focused less on details of destruction and judgment and more on hope. It is focused not on predicting the future but on living today out of a confident vision of God's future. The claim to be able to interpret

The Revelation literally (ha!) as a description of exact historical events in the future is a misuse of that book and of scripture generally.

Revelation uses a sort of coded language common in what are called "apocalyptic" writings (the book of Daniel is another example of an apocalyptic writing). Certain sayings attributed to Jesus in the Gospel accounts are apocalyptic.[17] The word means, loosely, "that which will be revealed." Thus, the original Greek name of the book of Revelation is "The Apocalypse." Apocalyptic language is intentionally metaphorical. It uses vivid imagery to make a particular point and to engage the reader at a deeper level of one's imagination,[18] and it has been highly successful judging by the reactions it has engendered over the years.

Revelation was written to specific churches in Asia Minor, to Christians experiencing persecution by those in power. These Christians were a distinct, despised minority within the culture. Conflict existed within and around these churches. It was not easy to be a Christian. There was a very real question of survival for these churches and how long they would be able to endure the adversity they were experiencing.

Revelation is a pastoral letter intended to encourage these congregations by pointing to a future in which God's kingdom comes on the earth, and peace and justice reign on earth. John gives a detailed, metaphorical description of how this will happen. The listeners to John's letter would have understood that the symbols he used (for example, the Antichrist and New Babylon) referred to people and places in their own history, such as Caesar and Rome. Additionally, the book of Revelation contains more references from the Old, or First, Testament than any other New, or Second, Testament writing. The message of hope was that Jesus, when he returns, will redeem the faithful, fulfill Israel's destiny through the church (the "adopted sister" of Israel), and bring a time of peace in which there are no tears or suffering. If a good story is judged by how dramatic and bloody it is, then Revelation meets the standard. Enemies are being defeated, and that's especially good when those enemies are people who have all the power over you in the present moment.

How do Presbyterians today interpret Revelation? How do we today receive this letter, which was intended to assure persecuted first-century Christians that their enemies would not be victorious in the end? We do not believe the letter is intended as a help or guide to identifying particular historical events in the present as the very developments "predicted" by John long ago. We do not believe it is a proper use of scripture to paint an image of a "vengeful Jesus," very different from the one we encounter in the

Gospel stories. We do not believe the Revelation to John is intended to scare us into following God by playing on our human fears of punishment and vengeance from God.

We do believe that the Revelation to John is intended to give us hope for the future.[19] We do believe it points to the truth that God will not ultimately be thwarted in bringing a kingdom of peace and justice in the world. We do believe Revelation is intended to call us to a new way of life reflecting a very different reality from the one we often see in the world around us. Presbyterians do believe God is always faithfully seeking redemption, mercy, justice, and love as revealed and known through Israel and in Jesus.

APOCALYPSE OR SHALOM?

How then do we wrestle with questions of the end times and understand them properly within a Presbyterian viewpoint. First, let's explore more deeply an important biblical image in our tradition: the kingdom of God. This is a somewhat difficult image and one that can be misunderstood, especially since there are large numbers of Christians who have mistakenly equated God's kingdom with the United States of America,[20] while other Christians have mistakenly identified the United States government as the tool of the Antichrist.[21]

Due to such potential for misunderstanding, a number of people, for various reasons, use different terms for the idea of the "kingdom of God." The "reign of God" implies a more dynamic and progressing description of God's rule as not just "a place" ("kingdom" can imply a geographic place), but an activity going on today as well as in the future. Since "kingdom" is a rather archaic term and is representative of earlier times in history, some have used the term "God's dream," which beautifully implies the idea of God's blessed intentions for the world. Another interesting metaphor used in place of kingdom is the "reality of God." This phrase describes in an interesting (almost science fiction) concept of how God's reality is not our own reality, though God's reality permeates everything around us. Still others use the term "commonwealth of God" to communicate how God calls human beings to a partnership of shared "governance" and care taking. The earth is the Lord's, yet the Lord calls people to be colaborers and faithful steward-partners in the resources and relationships of life on earth.

Whatever we choose to call the "kingdom of God," we cannot overstate the importance of this concept for Jesus and the early church, which thought of itself as a colony of God's kingdom here on earth.[22] The concept of God's kingdom, by whatever name, appears in the prophetic books of the Old, or First, Testament, that speak of a time when justice shall come to earth, when swords will be beaten into plowshares,[23] and a kingdom of peace will reign for all God's creation. Jesus picks up this theme, consistently preaching readiness for God's kingdom. In his "first sermon," he states that this kingdom is at hand.[24] His message to all who can hear is "Repent for God's kingdom is near."[25] He talked of the kingdom of God being among us and that we should seek God's kingdom first above all things.[26] He compared it to a wedding feast, a party to which everyone is invited, even the strangers and beggars off the streets.[27] He described God's reality as the lost being found,[28] as a father who forgives two sons,[29] as sight for the blind and healing for the lame,[30] and as a reality in which those who mourn find comfort.[31]

Jesus' vision of God's reign is more than "fires of burning sulfur."[32] He incorporates the Old Testament concept of "shalom" to describe what God brings into the world. Shalom is peace, but in a sense deeper than the mere cessation of violence. Shalom is a concept of peace with justice. It is living in harmony with all creation together in joyful life. The early church believed that Jesus' life, ministry, death, and resurrection revealed the "inbreaking" of God's kingdom, which God would bring to completion in God's own time. Just so, when we speak of God's reign here on earth, we are pointing to the reality of God's peace permeating our world. We do not know exactly what that will ultimately look like, nor do we know when it will be. We just know it will be.

WHY WE HOPE!

Do Presbyterians believe the world is coming to an end? Yes and no. Yes, we believe that there will be a day when suffering and death will be no more.[33] Justice and peace among all people will exist and no one will go hungry because of our inhumanity to each other. Yes, we have hope in the future God creates today and tomorrow. No, we don't believe the lights of eternity will "go out" even if there were to be cataclysmic violence and destruction on earth. No, we don't expect an Armageddon in which Jesus becomes a vindictive warrior-king killing the enemy. God is bigger than our limited understandings.

We hope because we believe God is "up to something" in our midst. God is up to something in our world as God works for peace and justice among all people. Although it may be difficult to see, God is up to something even in violent places like Hitler's Germany, Selma of the 1960s,

Kosovo, and Rwanda. God is up to something in our own lives, leading us into God's reality/dream/commonwealth/kingdom. We are called to awaken to that movement and open our eyes and ears to what God is doing.

We hope because we know the future is not up to us! In Presbyterian fashion, we emphasize that it is God who saves. It is God who will redeem the world, not our own feeble, or strong-armed, human efforts. We have a responsibility to respond to God's activities in our midst, but our hope rests in God and not only in ourselves. It is God who brings in a new creation as we despair of the old. It is God who acts for the salvation of the world, where we are unsure of new possibilities.

We hope because, in our very human community called the church, we experience God's new reality. In the ways we care for one another and the poor and lost in the world, we point to God's coming kingdom. When we gather for the sacrament of the Lord's Supper, we are looking to a time when people shall gather around the Lord's Table and there shall be no racial or economic barriers between us. When we worship as a community, we are living toward the coming world where all live in joy and praise of our Creator. When we enjoy the party of the Spirit's fellowship together, we celebrate the coming kingdom when all shall enjoy the bounty of God's love. We hope because we know God's reign/dream/commonwealth/reality is near at hand, and this is a good thing.

So What Do *You* Think?

1. What are the odds this week (a) that you will be met by Jesus coming down from the clouds? (b) that you will be met by Jesus in the encounter with a person in need? (c) that you will not meet Jesus at all?

2. How would you respond to someone who says, "If Jesus is not coming down from the clouds, there's nothing worth being prepared for. I might as well live only for my pleasure"?

3. If there was a web site on the internet that could tell you the date the world will end, would you check it out? What if it could tell you the date of your own death, would you want to know? Why do you think Jesus teaches that it is not for human beings to know or speculate about "the day and the hour" of "the end times"?

Do Presbyterians Have Spirit, or Do They Just Drink Them?

DANCING IN THE AISLES

Kevin had spent Saturday night with his best friend, Steve, so he went to Steve's church with him that morning. It was a worship experience very different from his own Presbyterian Church's worship. People were clapping and dancing in the aisles, some people had their hands in the air waving them around and saying, "Alleluia." One or two people were even shaking on the ground and saying strange words that sounded like gibberish. When Kevin asked his friend about what was going on, Steve told him they were speaking in tongues. "Don't you have the Holy Spirit at your church?" Steve queried. "I have heard Presbyterians aren't ever filled with the Holy Spirit. You don't even like to pray in public." Kevin didn't know what to say. He thought it was kind of fun to dance in worship, but he knew the people in his church would have a heart attack if anyone even clapped, much less got out of their seat. "Do we have any Spirit?" he wondered to himself.

DO YOU SPEAK IN TONGUES?

For many in the neo-evangelical tradition,[1] the presence of the Holy Spirit is an essential sign of one's holiness and rightness with God. For some, the presence of the Spirit is signified by certain manifestations such as speaking in tongues and being "slain in the Spirit" (a kind of fainting). There is even a phenomenon today in which persons "in the Spirit" laugh uncontrollably (we experience this every time we watch Robin Williams!).

> "You shall love the Lord your God with all your heart, and with all your soul, and with all your mind, and with all your strength. [And] you shall love your neighbor as yourself."
> —Rabbi Jesus of Nazareth [2]

Worship in the neo-evangelical tradition is characterized with highly emotional moments and opportunities for expressing one's faith personally. "Altar calls" offer an opportunity for persons, usually in a state of strong emotions, to come forward and turn their lives over to Jesus. Praise joined with tears is a common experience.

This makes sense in the neo-evangelical tradition, considering the importance placed on personal conversion. With so much invested in this moment of salvation, no wonder worship becomes so filled with emotions. When people experience change, often from underlying circumstances that have been tragic or crisis producing, it is emotional! These moments can even be very inspiring and uplifting.

In fact, one of the strengths of "expressionist" types of neo-evangelicalism is the freedom of feeling and emotion expressed in worship. Much that people find attractive about the neo-evangelicals involves the emotional spirituality and inspiring music. In a jaded culture looking for emotional experiences, the neo-evangelical tradition provides a framework for "modern" human beings to touch and to express the deepest parts of their spiritual lives. We need worship, rituals, and music that touch our souls.

Indeed, when the Holy Spirit is truly present, people do experience something quite extraordinary. People need to experience something or someone larger than themselves. Call it transcendence. In addition to the need for experiencing transcendence, there is also a dimension of Spirit-experience that can only be described as joyful and fun. In fact, when the Holy Spirit first "descended" on the disciples, many who witnessed its manifestation thought the disciples were drunk.[3] The neo-evangelicals remind those of us in other parts of the church that, more often than not, the best expression of worship is dancing in the aisles.

But, at its worst, this tradition also can distort worship into a setting for emotional manipulation, as if the Holy Spirit could be invoked using certain words or techniques. Preachers may try to manipulate the feelings of their congregation to get more and more people to come forward during the altar call as if the success of worship is measured by how many souls are saved.[4] Preaching can be structured more for its emotional effect than its theological soundness, and music can be chosen more for the emotional effect it creates than for the aspect of faith it represents. In the worship of certain neo-evangelical fellowships, the "message" implied to the worship participants is that one's holiness is enhanced by one's ability to speak in tongues, as if there were a hierarchy of spiritual gifts among God's people. Put another way, the more spiritual gifts one manifests, the more one can suppose one is touched by God. In settings where worship and spiritual life are judged primarily on the extent and degree of emotional expression, most Presbyterians would say such worship and spiritual life run the risk of losing touch with the larger and more whole sense of God's Spirit.

The danger, ultimately, is that worship becomes more about human need than truly an act of worshiping God. It becomes more "me and my needs" than an event transcending our own particular egos. It is another dose of the sort of spiritual navel-gazing we already do all too well in our individualistic culture. Worship should touch our human concerns and feelings. It should incorporate those very human experiences in the worship of God. But human experiences are not ends in themselves. They serve a much larger purpose.

Presbyterians always understand worship and the movement of the Spirit to be communal. Worship is not just individual action but the work of a community of people seeking to express their awe and wonder and thanksgiving before the Creator of the universe. When the Holy Spirit descended on the early church, the Spirit did not come upon only one individual, but upon a community of people.[5] The Spirit isn't simply for personal consumption or advancement, but for the empowering of a community to witness to God's kingdom. Worship isn't about me and what I want and need. It is about a God who calls me to serve and who gives me the Spirit to do so.

So, in short, the answer to the question of whether Presbyterians believe in speaking in tongues is a very strong yes and no. Yes, we believe the Holy Spirit can do things in the community of God's people beyond our own imaginations. Included in various manifestations of the Spirit can be a kind of spiritual ecstasy that, we realize, can be "out of our control."

(Immediately many Presbyterian-types will sense a "red-flag," signaling uneasiness with strong emotion.) No, we don't believe the gift of this Spirit is a kind of spiritual baptism appreciated most by those gifted individuals whom God has deemed worthy above all others. Yes, we believe the Spirit equips the church by empowering the community with a variety of gifts;[6] and, no, we don't believe the Spirit intends for these gifts to be sole manifestations as ends in and of themselves.

In fact, Paul discusses this quite clearly in his writings to the church in Corinth.[7] Some in Corinth were experiencing rather dramatic spiritual manifestations, of which speaking in tongues was one. Paul makes it clear that the purpose of the Spirit's gifts is not for individual honors but for serving the community at large. One gift from God's Spirit is not greater than another, and when those who speak in tongues exhibit this gift, it should be in service to the community's witness to the world. If it does not build up the community, it is useless, unnecessary, and even destructive.

We can be guided by Paul's wisdom here. Speaking in tongues can be part of the many gifts experienced by a community for the service of God's kingdom in the world. As a display of the Spirit's presence, its purpose is to help the church fulfill its purpose in the world. God grants the Spirit to the church not for our own ego building or emotional satisfaction but for the commissioning of the community to be the body of Christ here on earth.

CAN THE PRESBYTERIAN FROZEN CHOSEN BE THAWED?

As stated before, the strength of many neo-evangelical groups is their comfort with emotion in the spiritual life. For Presbyterians, the label "frozen chosen" has often been applied as a joke about our discomfort with emotion. In most Presbyterian churches, worship is a rather staid affair, with a rote pattern of standing and sitting, of following a liturgy in a particular way and form. It has been said that Presbyterians can't worship without a bulletin in their hands. God help us if someone actually clapped in worship.[8] We do indeed seem to be frozen in our pews.

One reason for this particular characteristic in our churches is our emphasis on the intellect or the mental aspects of religious life. Presbyterians always have stressed loving God with our minds. We require of our clergy and seek for our laity a particular level of education, and there is a general expectation of sound scholarship in preaching and teaching.[9] Theological reflection and discussion play an important role in our churches. We value using our intelligence to further our spiritual understanding and life, but sometimes, in our focus on the mind, we forget the heart.

Another reason for our hesitancy in displaying our spirituality in public is Jesus' warning to avoid practicing one's piety in public. In the Gospel of Matthew, in the section called the Sermon on the Mount, Jesus warns his disciples not to practice piety before others so that others may see them. When you give to the poor, give in secret. When you pray, go to your room, shut the door, and pray in secret. When you fast, do not look dismal, but wash your face and comb your hair so that others may not see your fasting.[10] We understand that the spiritual life is not about who is considered pious in public, nor is it about being perceived as being particularly spiritual. Instead, one's spirituality and piety are very much about humility and simplicity of heart.

Unfortunately, our stress on the intellect has meant a suspicion of the emotions. In the end, this may be more cultural than anything else, but we have tended to put less focus on nurturing the emotional aspects of our spiritual selves. We have abandoned the heart to pursue the mind, when both are needed for a complete spirituality. As we realize our shortcomings in this area, we can explore more fully how our brothers and sisters in the neo-evangelical tradition can help us discover something more, even parts of our own tradition which, for whatever reason, got left behind some time ago.

The question of whether we can be thawed is an appropriate one, though somewhat unnecessary because there are signs God already is defrosting us. Many Presbyterian churches are exploring more feeling-rich elements in worship and music.[11] There are new liturgical resources such as a "Service for Wholeness and Healing" and a "Reaffirmation of Baptismal Vows" that help us claim and practice more emotionally expressive parts of our spiritual life.[12] Several authors have written to help readers reclaim the spirituality of our tradition and make that spirituality part of our common life as members of the church.[13] All these are noteworthy signs of the Spirit who is moving in our midst and calling us to a more complete love of God and our neighbor.

MOUNTAINTOP SPIRITUALITY OR VALLEY SPIRITUALITY?

In reclaiming our Presbyterian understanding of the spiritual life, we have come to realize that "spiritual" may mean to us something slightly different from what it means to our neo-evangelical brothers and sisters. To illustrate, let's look at a Bible story called "the transfiguration of Jesus," which is found in three of the Gospel accounts.[14] In this story, we are told that Jesus took Peter, James, and John up a mountain to pray. While they were praying, the disciples fell asleep. (We all are asleep in a symbolic way, aren't we?) When they "awoke," they saw a vision of Jesus with his face shining brightly, standing in glory with Elijah and Moses. This is a real spiritual high, though a little frightening.

Peter is so excited that he asks Jesus if he (Peter) can build three tents so they can all stay on the mountaintop. Peter was on a spiritual high, literally, and he wanted to stay there. But in the very next verses, we learn that Jesus and the disciples come down off the mountain and are met by a great crowd from which a man asks Jesus to heal his son.[15] Jesus doesn't stay on the mountain. He reenters the world of hurting people.

In many ways, this story is symbolic of two different understandings of the spiritual life: mountaintop spirituality and valley spirituality. Mountaintop spirituality celebrates particularly powerful and emotional faith-experiences. Many neo-evangelical traditions significantly focus "for the success of salvation" on this emphasis, particularly in the worship aspect of spiritual life. Here again, single moments in time play an important role in the religious life, moments of being on a spiritual high, which believers carry with them throughout their lives. Such experiences shape who they are and their understanding of who they are to be. They continue to seek, week in and week out, these spiritual mountaintops, and, like Peter, want to build their tents there.

Another biblical illustration of this kind of spirituality is that of Paul. According to the book of Acts, Paul was originally Saul of Tarsus, a Jew who persecuted and helped kill the early Christians.[16] But then, on his way to a city called Damascus to arrest any Christians there, he was struck down by a great light. A voice spoke to Paul out of the light. The voice was understood to be that of Jesus. Paul was struck blind by the light, and it wasn't until he later stayed at a Christian's house and was healed and filled with the Spirit that his vision returned. This is a powerful story of a spiritual high, a mountaintop experience of epic proportions. It is a radical conversion often referred to by many neo-evangelicals. For them, Paul serves as a metaphor for their understanding of God's powerful intervention in their lives.

Many Presbyterians, though, understand the greater portion of spiritual life as not living on the mountaintop. While some of us may have had powerful experiences of God, most of us would not claim to have been struck down by a great light, or heard the voice of Jesus, or seen a burning bush.[17] Most of us encounter God in rather ordinary ways. For many of us, God is experienced mostly in valleys, rather than on mountaintops, among people in pain and in need of healing. Reformed and Presbyterian-types might be characterized more by a valley spirituality than by a mountaintop type.

This sort of spiritual life is never lived out predominantly on the mountain but in the daily existence of relationships and responsibilities. Our spirituality is made up of the ordinary things of life, less about powerful experiences of conversion and more about the daily conversion of our lives to God. Grace is the everyday experience of God's sustenance and care, not only on the mountain but, most especially, in the valley of life.

It may be that Timothy, more than Paul, can be considered a model of this valley spirituality. Timothy was a young man nurtured in the faith by his grandmother and by his mother, and his is a faith that dwells in him passed down from generation to generation, a faith that is also a gift from God.[18] This valley spirituality understands the Spirit as infiltrating all aspects of our lives, even the most humdrum. Call it "grace-based." (You knew we would get that word in there, didn't you?)

A grace-based spirituality celebrates the daily gifts of God found in each moment of every day. God is found not only in the burning bush of the mountain but in the everyday, normal life, in the mundane realities of our living, and in the experience of serving God in our work and in our play. Like the bread we eat during a celebration of the Lord's Supper, God is present to us in the ordinary elements of life. The bread that we eat in communion is not extraordinary, yet it becomes a symbol of how God's grace comes to us in our daily bread. The bread is not changed. We are.

Presbyterians can reclaim this understanding of valley spirituality. We live out such faith in this world amid messiness and confusion. We do not live on the mountain. We live and act in the daily chaos of people lost and in pain. In the midst of this uncertainty we experience the Spirit's presence gifting us with God's love and mercy.

WHY WE ARE SPIRIT FILLED!

Do Presbyterians have the Spirit? Most certainly! Maybe not in the ways a majority religious culture would like to understand it, or maybe not in a particularly dramatic fashion, but Presbyterians experience the Spirit every day, and we give thanks for the gift of God's sustaining presence.[19] Ours is a grace-filled spirituality in which life is about giving thanks and appreciating what God has done with us and among us. We are filled with the Spirit, and we drink of the Spirit of God's life poured out for us and in us. We embrace the goodness of life even in its ordinariness. This is what it truly means to be "awake in prayer."

In Alice Walker's novel *The Color Purple*, Celie is a woman beaten down both by her husband and by life circumstances. She has been despairing of ever knowing the goodness of life, being all but dead in the spirit. Then she meets another woman who has a grace-based spirituality. This woman transforms the way Celie looks at the world around her. In a letter mailed back to her sister Nettie, Celie tells Nettie that God gets "pissed off" if you "walk by the color purple in a field somewhere and don't [stop and admire the beautiful flowers God has made]."[20] God, according to Celie, feels shortchanged and miffed when God's people don't stop and celebrate God's relationship evident in the ordinariness of creation and life.

Don't leave God feeling shortchanged and miffed. Admire the color purple.

So What Do *You* Think?

1. Have you ever experienced personally or seen on television a service of worship that involved high emotionalism? If so, with respect for the people involved, describe what you saw and heard and what your thoughts were about it.

2. What guidelines would you offer to define when emotional expressions in worship are good and healthy and when they are not?

3. What did you think about the images in this chapter of "mountaintop" and "valley" spirituality? What kind of spirituality do you think most people have? What kind do you have?

4. Can you think of any times in your life when God has blessed you in seemingly "ordinary" encounters or events?

Why Don't You Repent in Dust and Ashes?

Underneath our clothes, we all are always naked.

Seventeen-year-old William was in his bedroom at 9:15 p.m. on Easter Sunday evening. He picked up the television remote control, thinking he would channel surf for a few minutes before he went over his notes for his three-minute presentation in speech class the next day. After brief stops on channels offering dated cartoons, sitcoms, movies, music videos, and a major league baseball highlight show, he stopped switching long enough to watch a broadcast from a church sanctuary (or "worship center").

There were no lilies visible, so William wondered if this might be a tape-delayed broadcast from some previous week rather than this morning's service. Perhaps because it was Easter night, William found the preacher's words rather depressing in tone. He began the sermon by reading from various newspaper accounts of multiple murders, child abuse, spouse abuse, and adultery. It sounded to William as though this speaker was in a debate class arguing either for the proposition "Sin is rampant," or against the proposition "The world is basically good."

William watched longer than he originally intended, and longer, honestly, than he wanted. He watched long enough for the preacher to repeat previous points of his outline after each next point was explained. "I am persuaded," he said each time, "(first) in the sinfulness of human beings, (then) in the holiness of God, (then) in the atoning blood of Jesus Christ, and (then) in the regenerative power of the Holy Spirit." William surfed on to a news channel and a weather channel before he punched the "off" button and opened his folder to his own speech notes for the next day.

Twenty minutes later, after he'd brushed his teeth, turned back his bed-covers, lain down, and turned off his study lamp, William stared at the dark ceiling wondering about the contrast between the Easter service he'd attended that morning on the lawn of the neighborhood Lazarus Come Forth Presbyterian Church and the TV preacher's "I am persuaded . . ." outline for his thirty-minute sermon.

He could tell from the Sunday night broadcast that the people in the pews of that church were attentive to their pastor's preaching. He'd also observed attentiveness on the part of the Lazarus Come Forth group that morning, but the service was substantially different: a community prayer of confession, scriptures related to the disciples going to the burial garden and discovering the tomb empty. There had not been a sermon, as such, at that sunrise service, but the pastor had invited the worship participants to speak about meaningfulness they had perceived over the years by God's grace in Jesus, crucified and resurrected.

William felt more "at home" with the service at Lazarus Come Forth Church. "But why?" he thought. "Ought I to be more persuaded, like that preacher, of the sinfulness of human beings, etc.?" He didn't want to "be more persuaded" exactly in that way, but "Should I?" he thought as his eyelids fell shut in sleep.

ARE YOU A SINNER?

If William has been to any Presbyterian worship services at all (and he has), he knows that Presbyterians believe all people are sinners. The Westminster Shorter Catechism (1649) gives a definition of sin as "any want [lack] of conformity unto, or transgression of, the law of God" (the response to question 14) and further states the extent of sin to include "the guilt of [humanity's] first sin, the want [lack] of original righteousness, and the corruption of [our] whole nature, . . . together with all actual transgressions which proceed from it" (the response to question 18). Some might say, "That about covers everything!" And they'd be right!

So, yes, if asked, "Are you a sinner?" all Presbyterians respond, "Absolutely I am; and so is every other person." Presbyterian-types believe, without qualification, that people are sinners. Yet many Presbyterians also convincingly raise questions about whether creation was ever pure and "perfect" and whether human beings "in the beginning" actually were pure and sinless. "Eden" and "The Fall" (Genesis, chapters 2, 3, and 4) may be a story illustrating a way to understand the difference between God and humanity in every age.[1]

Related to such questions and interpretations, neo-evangelicals and others sometimes comment that Presbyterians speak persuasively about sin being everywhere, but really are "soft on sin." So the question legitimately arises: Don't Presbyterians believe in sin?

Many Presbyterian critics ask this question because they perceive that Presbyterians are not as focused on "sin" as they (the critics) are. We could answer this question as we answered the question "Do you believe in the Bible?" No, Presbyterians don't believe in sin. We believe in the Lord of heaven and earth, but we're thoroughly convinced of the existence of sin.

The early generations of Reformed-Presbyterian folk understood sin as pervasive and, therefore, contaminating every part of our humanness, even our best and most loving of intentions. (See the Westminster Shorter Catechism, response 18, above.)

"Hellfire and brimstone" preachers pleading for aisles full of repentant sinners have picked up a few pointers from the Reformed-Presbyterian notions of the "total depravity" of all people. In the words of Paul's letter to the Romans (3:23), quoted previously in chapter 5, "All have sinned and fall short of the glory of God." Many neo-evangelical types, however, imply that sin can, to a great degree, become a matter of the past. They often suggest that sin can be left behind—for the most part—relegated to the "unregenerate" past, the time before one accepts Jesus as Savior.

Many, if not most, neo-evangelicals acknowledge sin as a continuing factor in the life of "the saved" with "spiritual re-dedications" periodically needed. Even so, for many, if there's a recognition of sin after "accepting Jesus," that recognition is frequently limited to thoughts and acts of sinfulness that we recognize and from which we "need to stay clear," obviously "big sins" such as theft, illicit sex, murder, cheating, drug abuse, and the like. But what about sin we don't recognize? Is there abiding sin we might call "small" sin? Is unrecognized "small" sin in the life of Christians "still sin"?

Presbyterians take absolutely seriously the present tense of the verb "fall short" in the Romans 3:23 verse. Presbyterians and certain others believe that sin is a continuing factor in every part of every individual's life and every part of every group's life. Whether big and recognized or small and unrecognized, sin is part of every person's conscious and subconscious being, as well as one's actions, even the most loving and well-intended actions. The same is true for a group's efforts, be those groups church, gang, government, social, school, racial/ethnic, or civic.

The *Book of Order* of the Presbyterian Church (U.S.A.) characterizes one of the "great themes of the Reformed tradition" as being "the recognition of the human tendency to idolatry and tyranny. . . ."[2] In other words, Presbyterians are absolutely convinced that all of us as humans "pledge allegiance" to choices we make. We "pledge allegiance" to influences, powers, and situations (often "good" influences, powers, and situations) with claims on us that are less than God's claim; therefore, day by day, we actually live as if God's claim is less than the others.

Presbyterians are convinced that sin is everywhere!

It is interesting that, in contrast to neo-evangelicals who believe Presbyterians are "soft" on sin because we don't preach God's "fire and brimstone" judgment enough of the time, philosophical and theological "liberals" often regard the Reformed-Presbyterian tradition as having an unhealthy, over-emphasized, obsessive preoccupation with sin!

It's always very tempting for any of us to think sin (of one sort or another) could not happen here. After the Murrah Federal Building was bombed in Oklahoma City in 1995, people in Oklahoma and across the United States said, "We would never have thought something like that could happen here." The same chorus was heard by residents of Littleton, Colorado, in 1999, when Columbine High School was devastated by a pair of gun-firing, bomb-planting students who murdered thirteen before committing suicide: "We would never have thought something like that could happen here."

In both instances, the sin of thinking a certain kind of sin could not surface in a given place was exposed by the sin of horrific violence, which obviously was possible all along. Three days after the Littleton, Colorado, tragedy, one anti-public school commentator interviewed on national television said, "You don't hear of things like this happening in private schools." Before noon on that same day, though, school officials at a Roman Catholic (private) school in Tulsa, Oklahoma, made public a web site created by a relatively small group of students at the school that contained written threats against certain fellow students and faculty members. Murder had not taken place at the private school, and those guilty of the threats said, "It was a joke," but one anti-public school commentator was shown guilty for the sin of thinking sin is limited to places other than his place of preference.

Daniel Migliore summarizes Reformed-Presbyterian "paradoxes" of sin: (1) Sin is both a "universal condition" and a "self-chosen act" for which individuals and groups are responsible; (2) sin is part of all human action, both what's identified as evil and what's perceived as good; (3) sin corrupts individual persons and corporate structures.[3]

Yet some neo-evangelicals and others wonder if Presbyterians, who believe sin is everywhere, actually believe anything much at all about sin. Reformed churchman and teacher John Leith has noted that the "distinctive theology of the Reformation" from Luther and Calvin rose from their common belief that, in spite of the seriousness and pervasiveness of sin in human life (individually and corporately), God still calls people by grace to new life and service. One side of this coin is that human ability does not make us new. The other side of the same coin is that sin does not disqualify us from God's relating to us over and over and over.[4]

While Presbyterians believe that sin is everywhere and that we either are continually attracted to or end up serving various "idolatries" and "tyrannies," we are equally convinced that God is not finished with us. God has callings of value for us in life, sinners though we always are.

SELF-RIGHTEOUS OR SELF-ACCEPTING?

Given the Presbyterian understanding of sin and grace, there's a choice: Will we be self-righteous or self-accepting? We know that we cannot presume we are ever without sin (1 John 1:8). To presume, at any point in life, even when "trusting God" and "accepting Jesus," that one is free of sin is, tragically, to be self-righteous (Luke 18:9–14).

If we agree with the saying "Underneath our clothes, we're all always naked," one might say, then, "The goal is to wear clothes to cover the nakedness." Someone from a nudist community, of course, would argue, "If we're all always naked, we might as well not wear clothes."

It's true, nakedness (or humanness) is not the same as sinfulness. Yet, if we are to be faithful to God, we cannot either ignore our sinfulness (as a nudist ignores nudity) or be preoccupied in covering our sinfulness (as more traditional clothes-wearers cover nakedness).

Confession is the statement recognizing and acknowledging an attitudinal turning away from sin, and repentance is what we call this turning of attitude from sin to God. In repentance, confessing sin is the antidote that keeps people from the dual dangers of either ignoring sin or trying to hide it. Presbyterians often confess sin together in worship, reading printed prayers, then continuing confession to God in silent prayer.

According to the Gospels, Jesus was often "on a tear" against self-righteousness, which is the ignoring or the covering of one's sin. That's all done with attitudes, rationalizations, and opinions. Repentance and confession, therefore, cannot be once-in-a-lifetime experiences. To use neo-evangelical terms, "inviting Jesus into one's heart" on one particular day does not eliminate the need to repent and confess from day to day to day.

Still, there is more to this sin-repentance-confession routine. The God who judges human sinfulness and forgives human sinfulness is continually choosing to work with God's people every day. Instead of being depressed, discouraged, or guilt-burdened about sin in its many forms, God calls us daily to participate in the new life we are told is possible through God's promises to Abraham and Sarah, to their descendants, Israel, and in the "person and work" of Jesus.

William wondered why he preferred the Easter sunrise prayers, hymns, and scripture at Lazarus Come Forth Presbyterian to the television preacher's "I am persuaded" sermon. Much of the difference between the two is "style." Any person's preference for one or the other could be based on personal "taste," being more drawn to one or the other. The negative side of the "I am persuaded" preacher's style is conveying the impression that if "you'll take my answer, you can get your off-track life back on track."

The style of the Easter sunrise service William had attended acknowledges human sinfulness, then encourages each person to consider who we are as people of God, the God who knows, loves, meets, calls, heals, sacrifices for, and gives grace to us all so that we may live lives made new day by day with all others. The worship service encouraged William to accept himself as: (1) a child of God; (2) a sinner needing and able to repent daily; and (3) a brother of other human beings on whom God has also not given up.

Self-acceptance in the gospel is the alternative to self-righteousness. Such self-acceptance does not ignore that sin is everywhere all the time. Such self-acceptance trusts God to continue working with us all, calling us all daily to repentance and confession for the purposes of creating love, justice, forgiveness, sacrifice, peace, wholeness, and so forth. God does this through us and others, sinners though we always are.

In the story of Job, when Job says to God that he (Job) "despises" himself and will "repent in dust and ashes" (Job 42:6), the traditional interpretation is that Job, in relation to God and in Job's own understanding, accepts a humanity drained and void of self-worth. At least one different interpretation, though, translates "despise" as indicating that he (Job) is admitting before God how he now understands both God's sovereignty and his own humanity in a way different from before. The Hebrew word traditionally translated "despise," might also be translated as "I see/hear/understand."

From chapters 38 through 41 of Job, God, speaking to Job, has argued that God is holy and that it's at least inappropriate for any human to know "all about God." Job, according to God, is human, but Job's humanity is no reason for surrendering the integrity of his humanity to life's agonies. God never disrespects or disdains Job for Job's anguished questions. Following this face-to-face hearing with God, Job "understands" anew and repents "of" (not "in") the self-pity and attitude of remorse ("dust and ashes") in which he was tempted to remain.[5]

God's conversation with Job and that story's conclusion also "justify" Job without his (Job's) surrendering to the theology of the "friends/arguers/preachers" who tried to convince him that some unrecognized sin was the cause of God's punishing him with tragedy. Job's friends were not correct, though Job had a relationship with God that needed attention.

So do we all. Biblical and spiritual self-acceptance is never satisfaction either with suffering in the world or with sin in our lives. Biblical and spiritual self-acceptance realizes and believes (1) that neither the world nor we as people are ever without sin and (2) that God is continually working with us for God's holy purposes, whatever happens in life or in death all around.

WHY WE HONOR ALL PEOPLE!

Leviticus 19:15–18 teaches both about love of neighbors, neighbors with whom you do not always "get along very well," and about love of self. Jesus quotes from Leviticus 19:18 (Matthew 22:34–40) and, in at least one instance, specifically adds love of enemies to the teachings on "love of neighbor" (Matthew 5:43–46). This perspective on God, sin, and humanity led John Calvin and others in Geneva, Switzerland, to fashion these two questions and responses as part of the Geneva Catechism:

Question: What do you understand by the term neighbor?

Response: Not only kindred and friends, or those connected with us by any necessary tie, but also those who are unknown to us, and even enemies.

Question: But what connection have they with us?

Response: They are connected by that tie by which God bound the whole human race together. This tie is sacred and inviolable, and no person's depravity can abolish it.[6]

How much William's theology and faith actually differ from the neo-evangelical preacher on television with the "I am persuaded" sermon on sin and salvation we cannot know, unless we were to ask that pastor some

direct questions. Yet William's instincts in preferring the Easter sunrise service at Lazarus Come Forth Presbyterian Church are very biblical instincts.

So What Do *You* Think?

1. Do you think it would be a good thing or a bad thing if the
idea of "sin" disappeared from our awareness? Why?

2. In the Bible, the man Job has a heartfelt dispute—perhaps
even an argument—with God. Tell, write, sketch, sing, or mime
about an experience when you, like Job, had a heart-to-heart discussion with God.

Who's in Charge?

PRAYING FOR YOU

Sarah and Khalid are juniors at John and Thurgood Marshall High School. Over a six-week period, they've been out together for one dance, a couple of movies, and an evening of skating. One afternoon, at her locker, after the day's last bell, Sarah noticed her friends Sherry and Bill approaching. "How's it going?" Sarah greeted them.

"Great," they said, almost in one voice.

"Sarah," Sherry began, "Bill and I want you to know that you and Khalid are in our prayers."

"Thanks," replied Sarah, "but is there something I should know that I don't know right now?"

"We're praying that you'll lead Khalid to a personal relationship with Jesus," Bill said.

"I didn't know that it's necessary for me to do that," Sarah responded, somewhat puzzled. "Why are you guys worried about this? I'm a Christian and Khalid is a Muslim. If that's okay for us, can't that be okay with y'all?"

"But," said Sherry, "John 14:6 quotes Jesus as saying, 'I am the way, the truth, and the life. No one comes to the Father except by me.' Our preacher says Christians shouldn't date non-Christians."

"So?" replied Sarah, still puzzled, a little irritated, and feeling some pressure from these two she'd known for ten years. "I'll pray about it. Thanks for your concern," she added as she closed her locker and headed to catch the bus. "Oh," she turned to add, "what's interesting to me is that Khalid's uncle tells him the same thing about dating non-Muslims that your pastor tells you about dating non-Christians." As Sarah turned and departed to board the bus, Sherry and Bill looked at one another, not knowing what else to say.

In the story above, Sherry and Bill (possibly without realizing it) are essentially saying, "Shouldn't you believe what my preacher says?" Sarah's short answer to this question could be "No." Her longer and less blunt answer could be "Not necessarily." And her still longer answer could be, "I shouldn't even believe what my own preacher says."

We already know Sarah is a human being (duh!). She has the capacity and ability to make decisions about her relationships and about her values and her faith. Let's say Sarah is also a Presbyterian. If she really is a Presbyterian, she certainly is on solid ground by resisting the spiritual pressure of her well-meaning friends. But what about any faith-based decisions she may make, similar to or different from Bill and Sherry?

DO PRESBYTERIANS BELIEVE IN ANY AUTHORITY?

Sarah may not be at all interested in the Presbyterian Church's understanding of decision-making. But if she is, a legitimate beginning question is whether Presbyterians believe in any authority over personal ethical choice and decisions. Sarah's friends, who seem to have been taught that their pastor's opinion is authoritative for church members' decision-making, might be wondering something like this, especially if Sarah ever tells them she is a Presbyterian and she doesn't necessarily even accept her own pastor's opinion as being exactly what she ought to do.

If Sarah is looking for some guidance in making certain decisions, for example, about her friendship with Khalid, there are "Presbyterian-type

building blocks" from which she can con-
struct her decisions; or, put another way,
there are "Presbyterian-type threads" from
which she can weave her decisions. Some
of these are based on Reformed and
Presbyterian understandings of: (1) human
beings as created by God, with much in
common and with much uniqueness; (2)
people, the world, and the church as
organic and connected; and (3) sin and
grace as related to the vocation (the "calling") of humans to serve as
God's stewards.

*God works even through
Presbyterian committees.*

Let's explore these three blocks for building, or threads for weaving, a
process of decision-making as Presbyterians.

1. *Human beings are created by God with commonality, uniqueness, and
diversity.*
Created by God, persons and groups may have much in common
with certain others, even with many others. Also, each person and
each group, in the infinite variety of God's universe, is unique. We
call that "diversity." Diversity, as an aspect of God's wisdom in creation, is to be appreciated and honored.

In the preceding chapter, we noted that all human beings are all
always sinners. That never means that all sins are equal in the effects
or outcomes they have, but that all people are equally immersed in sin.

This "sinfulness of all believers" is the counterpoint to the
often-mentioned Protestant understanding of the "priesthood of
all believers." The priesthood of all believers has been commonly
understood to mean that a clergy person is not required as a spiritual intercessor, or priest, in order for a "regular" person's prayers to
be heard and received by God. Some have alleged that Presbyterians
do not fully believe in the priesthood of all believers because
Presbyterians require an ordained clergy for the administration of
the sacraments of baptism and the Lord's Supper. Presbyterians,
however, are emphatic that the clergy, while trained in Bible, theology, and the care of people, are not up any notches on the spiritual
ladder or do not have any sharper spiritual ears to discern God's
whispers more accurately than anyone else; neither can it be said
that regular church members are down any notches on the ladder
from the clergy.

In other words, yes, Sarah—a person created by God both unique and with much in common with others—is perhaps younger and less experienced in life than many other people, but God has given her a mind and a personality for learning and for informed decision-making as much as God has given the same to Bill and Sherry and their pastor. Moreover, God will still be working with Sarah next month, next year, next decade, and throughout her life, beyond and through any decision she makes today and tomorrow, whether her decisions in any given day are more faithful or less faithful, whether her decisions work out well or not so well. This continuing effort and work of God with God's people brings us to the next "building block" or "thread for weaving," which is that . . .

2. *People, the world, and the church are both organic and connected.*
The word "organic" means more than "alive." Organic includes the process of evolving and changing from one stage, phase, or chapter in life to another, for example: conception, birth, physical development, biological and chemical alterations, learning, endings, death, and different (or new) beginnings, and so on.

"Organic" and, more particularly, "the process of evolving and changing" should not be associated (at least not for Presbyterians) with "spiritual" progress in the relationship between humans and God. Granted, one may argue that from walking (in one era) to space travel (in another era) is "progress," or that from using plant roots, leaves, and tree bark for medicinal purposes in one location or time period to using synthetic antibiotics in another location or time period is "progress." Most Presbyterians, however, will not concede in any argument that people are any less sinners in one time or place than another. We're all always sinners, yet this organic aspect of life—as God has created—continually makes possible an evolving, changing, and maturing of any person's relationship with God and an evolving, changing, and maturing of the church's ministry efforts.

Sarah's friendship (whether romantic or not) with Khalid provides an example of a person's relationship to God and to God's people that illustrates commonality, that expresses uniqueness and diversity, and that always has organic dimensions. The possibility exists that Sarah will grow, evolve, change, and mature as a person, and that this will happen through her learning and considerations with respect to her relationship with Khalid and with others.

Should Sarah be a Presbyterian, though, who looks to the church for guidance in decision-making, it's crucial to understand an element of creation in addition to each person or group having much in common with others, in addition to each person or group being unique and diverse, and in addition to the life of each person or group having organic dimensions. That additional element is the connectional nature of people, the world, and the church.

While we generally are aware that persons and groups are interrelated, from automobile owners and coffee drinkers in the United States to oil producers in the Middle East and coffee growers in Central or South America, Presbyterians (and certain other faith-traditions) go a step further, believing that, as the church is a corporate body, people associated as "church" have a connected relationship.

As one theologian has put it: "There can be no church without local congregations and no local churches except as they participate in the universal church."[1] Presbyterians, convinced that this connectionalism is important, practice ministry through the church: (a) recognizing and honoring Jesus Christ as head of the church and as the complete revelation of God's involvement with God's people (noted particularly in chapter 4);[2] and (b) recognizing and honoring the elements of debate, agreement, and disagreement among God's people, as much in the church as in the world.

Presbyterian-types have encouraged and continue to encourage debate, agreement, and disagreement because:

- We have believed that God calls each of God's people to a faithful stewardship of each one's mind and relationships, since "faith and practice, truth and duty" go together;[3]
- We have believed that "God alone is Lord of the conscience" when any persons or groups have advice or opinions that conflict with scripture;[4]
- We have believed that laypersons and church governing bodies do make errors at times and do act wrongly whenever pressuring people to "go along" with a given interpretation or ruling, with which those being pressured do not agree (such pressure is called "binding the consciences" of others, and it's wrong because church "power" rightly is "ministerial and declarative," that is, serving and proclaiming in its nature, not coercive and manipulative);[5] and

- We have believed that God is leading God's people to be engaged "in, with, against, and for the world" according to God's love and call in Jesus Christ.[6]

This connectional nature of the church is not a cemented nature. Rather, it's the result of our being created by God with much in common and with much uniqueness and diversity, as well as being created by God with organic and connected characteristics.

3. Sin and grace are related to our vocation ("calling") as God's people "in, with, against, and for the world."
This means the God who, in grace, creates the universe, the earth, people, and so forth, also, in grace, redeems and makes human life new continually. Sin is always everywhere, and in spite of sin, God's grace is present continually. (Grace is the word!) Because of grace, then, vocation ("calling") is never what a person does to earn a living but always how one lives serving God every day in life. If vocation ("calling") is how one lives serving God every day of life, that makes God's people "stewards" in God's world, called to faithful stewardship of every part of life, including working, volunteering, decision-making, studying, relaxing, learning, being a friend, and so forth, while being shaped daily by God's Word and Spirit.[7]

We're now ready to ask: If Presbyterian-type "blocks" for "building decisions" or "threads" for "weaving decisions" include these parts (the way God creates with commonality, uniqueness, and diversity; the way God creates persons, church, and world as organic and connected; and the way God, by grace, calls God's people to a whole-life vocation of stewardship), what considerations can contribute to Sarah's decision-making about her friendship with Khalid?

We presume Sherry and Bill and their pastor would have in mind Jesus' frequently quoted verse "I am the way, and the truth, and the life. No one comes to the Father except through me" (John 14:6).

Sarah, with the assistance of her pastor, or without, could study John's Gospel to learn that a clear anti-Jewish bias existed among many Christians in the time the account was written, possibly fifty years after Jesus' death and resurrection (such a bias comes through, for example, in John 14:6). That fact, however, does not mean either that Jesus did not say it or that the theology of the statement might not be true, though in a way different from the way many interpreters have tended to interpret it. Usually, this verse has been interpreted as being a "weeding out" declaration by Jesus. In other words, Sherry and Bill's pastor believes Khalid needs to "accept Jesus as Lord and Savior" because otherwise Khalid won't have a prayer for eternal life in God's presence. (God "won't let him in" except as Jesus approves him.)

But what if it's true in another way? What if the truth here, in a century different from the time in which it was written, is not a bias against Jews and other non-Christians? What if the truth here lies in Jesus' being the Good Shepherd, the Gatekeeper, the Messiah-Redeemer who allows into God's presence all who recognize God's way, truth, and life, but with some of those who recognize God's way, truth, and life being people who live and interpret differently from others? In that case, the voice of the One who is "the way, the truth, and the life" sounds different to some in different centuries and cultures than that voice sounded to John who recorded this particular Gospel account, and it possibly sounds different from how any of us hear that Good Shepherd's voice.

Reformed/Presbyterian-types have, for centuries, been reluctant to declare whom God has "chosen" and whom God has "not chosen."[8] Moreover, increasingly Presbyterians have been recognizing that a clear study of scripture means seeking to hear God's voice in scripture while, at the same time, identifying potentially unhealthy biases that are mixed into the texts of the Bible. This means seeking to be guided by the still living Word heard in the written words of the Bible.[9]

Sarah may conclude, in good faith, that Jesus is the way, the truth, and the life of God, not only for her and for professed Christians, but for all. She may further conclude, though, that certain representations of Jesus by certain well-meaning, self-proclaimed representatives of Jesus do not help her make decisions that she believes are most faithful to the God whom she's come to know in Jesus.

If Sarah decides through study and discussions and prayer that Khalid need not be converted to Christianity for him to be worthy as her friend (or spouse) in the eyes of God, she can make that decision "on good authority" in the Reformed and Presbyterian traditions. She can make that decision still respecting, but without having to agree with, the faith convictions of Bill, Sherry, their pastor, or Sarah's own pastor.

CHURCH PROFESSIONALS OR A PROFESSING CHURCH?

If Sarah happened to be a Presbyterian, and if Presbyterians are recognized as being able to make decisions of conscience through prayerful considerations of scripture, history, science, church confessional statements, and the wisdom of other people, then how do Presbyterians understand church authority in relation to the clergy? Put another way, do we understand our most faithful witness to depend on "church professionals"? Presbyterian theologian Daniel Migliore summarizes some general observations against "church" and church "professionals" (who could be clergy or members):

1. The tendency to promote spiritual individualism or to surrender to cultural individualism;
2. The tendency to cater to individual members and to almost privatized, homogeneous groups (groups wherein members are quite similar in their opinions, backgrounds, current life situations, etc.);
3. The tendency to develop and maintain structure that supports existing rules and "rulers";
4. The tendency to tolerate (and even promote) a spirituality and discipleship that "talks the talk" but does not faithfully "walk the walk" of God with Israel and in Jesus.[10]

Presbyterian-types, at their best, encourage church professionals and church officers prayerfully to develop a deep and authentic spirituality for discipleship and leadership. (Sarah may have known her pastor and church officers to be this way.) There's an equal emphasis for all members to do the same, Sarah included; and, as her comments indicate, she at least somewhat realizes this.[11]

When development of spirituality for discipleship and leadership occurs day by day, from generation to generation, one group of God's people will be observed by others to be more a professing church than one predominantly relying on the pronouncements of church professionals.

WHY WE DO IT DECENTLY AND IN ORDER!

It has been said of Presbyterians, "They do (church) decently and in order." Some would say that makes Presbyterians obsessed with too many rules, too much legalese. A lawyer is required to figure out the system. To some degree, this may be true, but the purpose behind the orderliness is to encourage the mutual ministry of Jesus Christ.

Because Presbyterians work in mission in community, we do not make up the rules as we go along. This practice is rooted in the understanding that, in our relationships, God prefers order to chaos or manipulation. Of course, this never eliminates sin or human error within the church, which are always with us, even at some (or many) meetings of Presbyterian groups! At times, we admit, people manipulate the process for their personal or political advantage. But Presbyterians believe that an orderly system of church government is the best way to ensure that conflict can get resolved and that the church can move toward new life. On the human side, there are checks and balances and oversight from the local church to the national assembly of the church. On the divine side, the Lord is at work among and through us.

Someone has said, "Presbyterians believe the Holy Spirit 'moves' through ordered groups."[12] In that "decently and in order" process of prayer, study, debate, deliberation, and voting, Presbyterians are convinced the church, by God's grace, can be open to and led by God's continuing call. Through the ages, people—we among them—are called and engaged as disciples and stewards of God's grace in every part of life, all to the glory of God.

So What Do *You* Think?

1. Picture in your mind three leadership styles: one that pressures too much, one that pressures too little, and one that's just right. Describe the styles, actions, and other qualities of each.

2. Read again the story of Sarah and Khalid. What do you think Sarah should do?

3. Suppose that someone running for President of the United States said that every decision a President makes should be based strictly on the Bible. Would this make you want to vote for this candidate or not? Why?

Epilogue

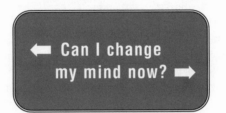

T he story is told of a soldier who was traveling through the coun-
tryside. He came upon a village square, dismounted, and got water
from the well for his horse and himself. As he was drinking, he
happened to notice a fence by a house covered with circles made of chalk.
And in the exact middle of each circle was an arrow. He was amazed by the
marksmanship of the archer who had shot the arrows with such precision.
He decided he needed to meet this marksman, and he began to ask some
of the villagers if they knew who had done such a wondrous thing. They
replied they did not. Finally after many inquiries, one villager mentioned
seeing a young girl with a bow and arrow. When the soldier found this
young woman, he inquired, "Are you the one who shot the arrows into the
circles?"

She shyly replied she was. He asked who had taught her to shoot so
well, and she said she had taught herself. "Could you show me how you did
it?" he asked. "Certainly," she responded. She took her bow and arrow and,
facing the fence, shot her arrow into the fence. Whereupon, she took a
piece of chalk out of her pocket and drew a circle around the arrow.

In many ways, we think that what we have done in this small volume
is simply draw circles around the arrows of Presbyterian beliefs. We have
tried to sketch in general terms the theological ideas that shape our heritage
and that point to the future. Each of us has been in conversation with the

other's theological beliefs, and together we've been in conversation with the faith considerations of others. In writing the book, we realize more than ever the dangers of drawing our circles of chalk too widely. It is always problematic when generalizing and simplifying concepts that persons of keener minds than ourselves articulate in finer detail.

In fact, one circle we run dangerously close to drawing too large is identifying the belief system of the neo-evangelical tradition. In striving to respond to ideas and convictions of that branch of Christianity, we paint in broad strokes a viewpoint much more complex than we could identify in these few pages. And, we must say again, all neo-evangelicals do not uniformly subscribe to the various theological positions we have sought to address as examples. We believe our description is accurate in general, but, as in all attempts to engage in conversation, we realize we have not fully described the nuances of their belief systems. We look forward to seeing the circles of chalk they draw around arrows they shoot.

As to the circles we have drawn around Presbyterian ideas, we know not all will agree with us, and they will let us know that. That is part of the fun of being Presbyterian. Yet we do believe fervently that Presbyterians must claim the strengths of our theological tradition in the face of a religious culture somewhat different from our own.

We believe we have identified certain basic elements important to our tradition, grounded both in the history of Israel and in the life, ministry, death, and resurrection of Jesus Christ witnessed to in the scriptures. In fact, these themes shape the framework of our tradition and remain consistent for us in any conversation we have with others or with ourselves. These words have shown up practically in every chapter of this book.

GRACE

This word above all words describes how Presbyterians understand themselves. In the simple, freely given giftedness of God's love in Jesus Christ, we have the truth of God's all-encompassing mercy and compassion. This grace is so radical we cannot fathom its totality, but we measure all assertions about God against this experience of grace. (We would deny any form of works' righteousness no matter how subtle a form it may come in.) At the heart of our disagreement with the neo-evangelical tradition is that they fail to see how emphasizing a specific decision by a human for salvation swings to the side of believing in our ability to save ourselves.

Grace affirms that it is God who acts and saves humanity. It is God who searches for us and finds us even when we, like Adam and Eve, would rather hide in the bushes to conceal our nakedness.[1] It is God who saves us when we cannot save ourselves. This is our hope, and belief, and faith. In a culture that values earning your way to the top and being in control of your destiny, it is a very radical assertion to believe in grace, but that is who we are.

GRATITUDE

Presbyterians understand that how we live our lives is always a response to the initial gift of God's love. Influenced not by fear or shame, but led by God's Spirit to live with gratitude and thanksgiving means valuing the gift given with a life that really never has been our own. The gift of God's love claims our lives and calls us to paths of service we may otherwise want to ignore. Gratitude is the essence of our morality; it is the basis for our spirituality; and it calls us to dance lives of servanthood. In a culture that is never satisfied, it is hard to live lives of gratitude, but that is who we are.

COMMUNITY

Presbyterians always understand that faith is to be lived out among a diverse community of people. We cannot separate our salvation from the struggles of our brothers and sisters in faith. Christianity is not an enterprise of rugged individualists. We believe we need one another to live out the faith. We need a community of diverse people willing to engage scripture and one another in searching for God's will in our communal lives. We believe community is essential in witnessing to God's kingdom/reign/dream/commonwealth/reality. In a culture that values and promotes the individual person, it is not easy to find and live in community, but that is who we are.

HUMILITY

The final theme is one we began with. In the introduction, we articulated that for all Presbyterians, we feel compelled to be humble when we speak of faith. We always understand how our words fall short of God. This makes our theological reflections feeble human attempts at capturing the mystery of God beyond our comprehension. This challenges us to call into question anyone who tries to assert with zealousness the truth of their faith claims, overriding the faith convictions of another. We always understand our assertions to be an effort of a finite people living in a particular historical period. We are not God. So we must be willing to admit and explore the possibilities of our theological viewpoints being wrong. This is why Presbyterians are always open to changing their theological positions if so guided by the Spirit. We understand ourselves to be the church reformed, always being reformed.[2] In a culture that values certainty, it is not easy to live a faith willing to question itself constantly, but that is who we are.

YOUR TURN

It is our greatest hope that you will take the ideas of this book and explore how they intersect with your experience of God. It is our sincere hope you will continue the conversation shared here and take it to new and insightful levels. If you embrace the great tradition we have learned to love and cherish, we will certainly feel God has used our feeble attempts far beyond our expectations. We pray you now take the piece of chalk, and go out into the world, drawing your circles around God's grace-filled presence, the Presence that goes forth before us all. Amen!

Notes

INTRODUCTION

1. Speaking at a national Presbyterian Men's gathering in New Orleans the evening of May 1, 1987, then mayor of Atlanta, Andrew Young, began his speech by saying provocatively, "I want to explain how the world is in so much trouble and how you caused it." (See *Presbyterian Outlook* 169, no. 20 (May 25, 1987): 2.) With tongue in cheek, he then, more than once, repeated the phrase "You Presbyterians are the problem," referring generally to Presbyterians' ecumenical mission and service efforts that have been both national and international. Specifically, he referred to the positive influence in his own life when, as a young man, he attended a conference on a racially integrated church and society, which was sponsored, among others, by the Presbyterians.

2. Regarding the term "conservative," Presbyterians understand themselves (with others) to be those who conserve the essential beliefs of the Judeo-Christian faith through the ages. Additionally, Presbyterians are "evangelical" in the sense of being "messengers of the good news of God's redeeming love for the world." "Neo-evangelical," however, will be the term we use to describe a branch of Christianity prevalent in the Bible Belt and elsewhere. Neo-evangelicalism is characterized, at least since the early 1900s, by (1) a more fundamentalist and/or literalist interpretation of scripture, and/or (2) a more charismatic/Pentecostal expression of faith than is practiced by Presbyterian Church (U.S.A.) members generally.

3. The 1996 Muslim population in the United States is reported as 3.3 million in *The New View Almanac: Premier Edition* (Woodbridge, Conn.: Blackbirch Press,

Inc., 1996), 116; and as 5.1 million in *The World Almanac and Book of Facts, 1998,* ed. Robert Famighetti (Mahwah, N.J.: K-III Reference Corp., 1998), 651. Comparatively, Presbyterian Church (U.S.A.) membership since 1996 has been reported as slightly less than 3 million.

4. The whole of scripture is about God working to speak God's word through small minority communities from some slaves who lived in Egypt to (centuries later) some disciples in Palestine following a maverick rabbi named Jesus.

5. Theological Declaration of Barmen, *The Constitution of the Presbyterian Church (U.S.A.),* Part I, *Book of Confessions* (Louisville, Ky.: Office of the General Assembly, 1994), 8.01–8.28.

6. The Theological Declaration of Barmen was treasonous in that it declared any claim of ultimate authority by state or church to be a false claim. Dietrich Bonhoeffer and others were imprisoned and executed for the various avenues they pursued in opposing the Nazi regime. In other times and places, other religiously faithful persons also have been executed by opponents of their respective religious traditions.

7. Eberhard Busch, *Karl Barth: His Life from Letters and Autobiographical Texts* (Philadelphia: Fortress Press, 1976), 234–35. For further reading on "Jesus as a Jew," see also (1) Marcus Borg, *Meeting Jesus Again for the First Time: The Historical Jesus and the Heart of Contemporary Faith* (San Francisco: Harper Collins, 1994), 22; and (2) Russell Shorto, *Gospel Truth: The New Image of Jesus Emerging from Science and History and Why It Matters* (New York: Riverhead Books, 1997), 194–95.

8. Among others, Presbyterian minister the Reverend John Williams, serving as Director of Church Relations, Austin College, Sherman, Texas, has advocated "stewardship of the mind" as being consistent with the teachings of John Calvin, John Knox, and others in the 1500s, and of others in the Reformed/Presbyterian tradition since.

9. *The Constitution of the Presbyterian Church (U.S.A.),* Part II, *Book of Order* (Louisville, Ky.: Office of the General Assembly, 1994), G-1.0301 (noting that this is quoted from the Westminster Confession of Faith, *The Constitution of the Presbyterian Church (U.S.A.),* Part I, *Book of Confessions,* 6.109).

10. Through the twentieth century, the Presbyterian Church (U.S.A.) and her "predecessor denominations" have encouraged moderation in the practice of certain life options. In this, Presbyterians are well aware of the dangers inherent in alcoholism and of the health risks related to smoking. Members are encouraged to make wise choices. At this time, however, the church does not believe there can be too much dancing!

11. *The Constitution of the Presbyterian Church (U.S.A.),* Part II, *Book of Order,* G-1.0304.

12. Ibid., G-14.0207b and G-14.0405b.

CHAPTER 1. ARE YOU SAVED, OR ARE YOU PRESBYTERIAN?

1. The use of the terms "above" and "below" are not intended literally and, therefore, spatially. In the time of Jesus, the worldview of the universe understood heaven as being "up above" while hell was somewhere "down below." Today we understand these terms much more metaphorically. Certainly we don't interpret them as literal descriptions of the world's and the universe's arrangement. The essence of Jesus' expression here is that this new birth comes from God and not from us.

2. Baptism is one of the two sacraments recognized by the Presbyterian Church (U.S.A.) and by most Reformed/Presbyterian type churches. (See *Book of Order*, W-1.3033 (2).) Presbyterians understand sacraments to be visible signs of invisible grace. As the sacraments are celebrated, by God's grace, people experience the gift of God's presence and love known ultimately in Jesus Christ. "Baptism is the sign and symbol of inclusion in God's grace and covenant with the Church" (*Book of Order*, W-2.3004). This is one reason Presbyterian-types do not link salvation to baptism. A person's salvation is not dependent on one's baptism. The sacrament is the sign and symbol of being claimed and included by God. Neither the ritual nor the experience of baptism either creates salvation or bestows it. Remember the Presbyterian mantra: "God saves."

3. *The Constitution of the Presbyterian Church (U.S.A.)*, Part II, *Book of Order*, W-2.3007.

4. Matthew 9:9–13; Mark 2:14–17; Luke 5:27–32; 15:1–10.

5. Luke 15:11–32.

6. Romans 8:38–39.

CHAPTER 2. IS THE BIBLE THE LITERAL WORD OF GOD, OR JUST A LONG, BORING BOOK?

1. John H. Leith, ed. *Creeds of the Churches* (Atlanta: John Knox Press, 1973), 310.

2. John T. McNeill, *The History and Character of Calvinism* (London: Oxford University Press, 1954), 396–98, 403. The citations refer to John M'Leod Campbell and Charles A. Briggs, respectively. Also, for a thorough treatment of twentieth-century developments among United States Presbyterians, see Bradley J. Longfield, *The Presbyterian Controversy* (New York: Oxford University Press, 1991).

3. *The Constitution of the Presbyterian Church (U.S.A.)*, Part II, *Book of Order*, G-14.0207b.

4. See 1 Peter 2:18.

5. See 1 Corinthians 14:34–35.

6. Westminster Confession of Faith (chap. 1, para. 9), *The Constitution of the Presbyterian Church (U.S.A.),* Part I, *Book of Confessions,* 6.0009. For further study, see "Presbyterian Understanding and Use of Holy Scripture, Position Statement Adopted by the 123rd General Assembly (1983) of the Presbyterian Church in the United States" and "Biblical Authority and Interpretation, A Resource Document Received by the 194th General Assembly of the United Presbyterian Church in the United States of America" (Louisville, Ky.: The Office of the General Assembly, 1992). These two are printed together as booklet #OGA-92–003. Also see Shirley C. Guthrie, *Always Being Reformed: Faith for a Fragmented World* (Louisville, Ky.: Westminster John Knox Press, 1996), 24–29.

7. John B. Rogers, Jr., "The Book That Reads Us," *Interpretation* 39 (October 1985): 388–411.

CHAPTER 3. ARE YOU GOING TO HEAVEN, OR TO TULSA?

1. This in no way compares Tulsa, Oklahoma, to heaven or hell. However, some people might consider Tulsa to be a "geographic buckle" of a Bible Belt mentality because of the presence of neo-charismatic institutions such as Oral Roberts University and RHEMA Bible Church and Training Center.

2. "Jiggy" a term with rock and roll, rhythm, and rap associations, is borrowed from entertainer Will Smith's "Gettin' Jiggy Wit It," from the CD *Big Willie Style* (Sony Music Entertainment, Inc., 1997).

3. The characterization of heaven as a window for viewing hell is presented in the parable of the rich man and Lazarus (Luke 16:19–31). The parable's intent, however, is quite different from those who desire "heavenly box seats" to have a bird's-eye view of hell's inhabitants suffering as they deserve.

4. From *Marx's Criticism of the Hegelian Philosophy of Right: Introduction,* quoted in *The Macmillan Dictionary of Quotations* (New York: Macmillan Publishing Co., 1987), 474. Marx believed this, but he failed to see how religion could be a force for a great change in society, how it could wake people up to the possibilities of justice and peace. One has only to look at Gandhi and Martin Luther King, Jr., in the twentieth century to see the power of faith to change our world.

5. Hosea 1:2–3; 2:19–20.

6. Isaiah 66:10–11,13.

7. Nehemiah 9:17c.

8. Luke 15:1–32.

9. Matthew 22:23–33; Mark 12:18–27; Luke 20:27–38.

10. Romans 8:38.

11. 1 Peter 3:18–20a.

12. See Yaffa Eliach, *Hasidic Tales of the Holocaust* (New York: Oxford University Press, 1982).

13. See Isaiah 44:8; Jeremiah 1:8; Matthew 28:5; Luke 2:10.

14. 1 Thessalonians 5:16–18.

15. "The Shorter Catechism" *The Constitution of the Presbyterian Church (U.S.A.)*, Part I, *Book of Confessions*, 7.001.

16. "A Brief Statement of Faith," *The Constitution of the Presbyterian Church (U.S.A.)*, Part I, *Book of Confessions*, 10.5.

CHAPTER 4. IS JESUS "LORD," OR JUST A GOOD GUY?

1. Many Bible students, teachers, archaeologists, theologians, etc., have sought to clarify a difference between Jesus' identity in his life and ministry and later characterizations of his identity by "believers," using such terms as: (1) "the historical Jesus" and "the Jesus of faith"; (2) "the Jesus of history" and "the Christ of faith"; (3) "the Jesus of Palestine" and "the Jesus of multilayered traditions."

2. Matthew 1:21; see also Joshua 1:1–9.

3. See Bernhard Lohse, *A Short History of Christian Doctrine: From the First Century to the Present*, trans. F. Ernest Stoeffler (Philadelphia: Fortress Press, 1966), 37–99.

4. Bible students and teachers have long thought that Jesus' life and ministry were patterned after passages from the Hebrew scriptures/Old Testament. Some believe that the gospel account writers intentionally and interpretively told the Jesus stories reflecting themes from the Hebrew scriptures in order to illustrate Jesus' person and work. For one of the most provocative of these volumes, see John Shelby Spong, *Liberating the Gospels: Reading the Bible with Jewish Eyes* (San Francisco: Harper, 1996).

5. For a description of these three in much greater detail, see Gustaf Aulen, *Christus Victor: An Historical Study of the Three Main Types of the Idea of the Atonement*, trans. A. G. Hebert (New York: Macmillan Publishing Co., 1969).

6. Daniel L. Migliore, *Faith Seeking Understanding: An Introduction to Christian Theology* (Grand Rapids: William B. Eerdmans Publishing Co., 1991), 239.

7. John Calvin, *Institutes of the Christian Religion*, ed. John T. McNeill, trans. Ford Lewis Battles (Philadelphia: Westminster Press, 1960), II, viii, 55.

CHAPTER 5. ARE ONLY 144,000 SAVED?

1. Romans 11:34, where Paul paraphrases Isaiah 40:13.

2. For information on these with greater detail, under entries such as "Pelagianism," "Arminianism," etc., see *The Oxford Dictionary of the Christian Church*,

ed. F. L. Cross and E. A. Livingstone, 2d ed. (Oxford: Oxford University Press, 1974).

3. See John H. Leith, *John Calvin's Doctrine of the Christian Life* (Louisville, Ky.: Westminster/John Knox Press, 1989), 107–45.

4. For an outline of "The Five Points of Calvinism" from the Dutch Synod of Dort (1618–1619), "Total depravity; Unconditional election; Limited atonement; Irresistible grace; Perseverance of the saints" (*TULIP*), see McNeill, *History and Character of Calvinism*, 265.

5. See chapter 3 of the Westminster Confession of Faith, *The Constitution of the Presbyterian Church (U.S.A.)*, Part I, *Book of Confessions*, 6.014–6.021 (also 6.064–6.067).

6. Westminster Confession of Faith, *The Constitution of the Presbyterian Church (U.S.A.)*, Part I, *Book of Confessions*, 6.187–6.192.

7. *The Constitution of the Presbyterian Church (U.S.A.)*, Part II, *Book of Order*, G-2.0500(1).

8. For a few examples, see: Psalm 139:7–12; Jeremiah 29:1–32; 1 Peter 3:18–20a.

CHAPTER 6. WHEN WILL THE WORLD END, OR DID IT END IN THE 1960S?

1. Like the Messiah's forerunners, such as Elijah and John the Baptizer, Jesus was a male. So, as it was assumed before Jesus, it's been assumed since, that when the Messiah returns, the Messiah will be male. We have a suspicion, though, that God who either shatters or "sneaks around" human expectations may take exception to our assumptions. The Messiah, on return, may or may not look as we anticipate.

2. Hal Lindsey, with C. C. Carlson, *The Late Great Planet Earth* (Grand Rapids: Zondervan Publishing House, 1970).

3. See the fictional *Left Behind* series by Tim La Haye and Jerry B. Jenkins, (1) *Left Behind: A Novel of the Earth's Last Days*; (2) *Tribulation Force: The Continuing Drama of Those Left Behind*; (3) *Nicolae: The Rose of the Antichrist*; (4) *Soul Harvest*; and (5) *Apollyon: The Destroyer Is Unleashed* (Wheaton, Ill.: Tyndale House Publishers, Inc.)

4. See Shorto, *Gospel Truth*, 95.

5. Ibid., 62.

6. See Mark 13:30 and John 21:23.

7. 1 Corinthians 7:8–9, 25–31.

8. See, among others, (1) Clyde L. Manschreck, *A History of Christianity in the World: From Persecution to Uncertainty* (Englewood Cliffs, N.J.: Prentice-Hall, Inc., 1974), 214–15; and (2) James H. Smylie, "A New Heaven and a New Earth: Uses

of the Millennium in American Religious History," *Interpretation* 53 (April 1999), 143–57.

9. See Grant R. Jeffrey, *Armageddon: Appointment with Destiny* (Toronto: Frontier Research Publications, 1977).

10. Ibid., 184–86. Jeffrey's "candidate" for the Antichrist is a "revived Roman Empire" comprised of western, central, and southern European countries, many of which are historic allies of the United States and current NATO partners.

11. Matthew 24:3–31; Mark 13:5–27; Luke 21:7–36.

12. 1 Thessalonians 4:14–17.

13. Revelation 13:18.

14. See Revelation 16:16 and, among others, Bruce M. Metzger, *Breaking the Code: Understanding the Book of Revelation* (Nashville: Abingdon Press, 1993), 83–84.

15. Matthew 24:36.

16. Acts 1:7.

17. Matthew 24:29–31; Mark 13:24–27; Luke 21:25–28.

18. Metzger, *Breaking the Code: Understanding the Book of Revelation*, 11.

19. Ibid., 106.

20. Many scholars conclude that the drive behind the expansion and growth of the United States was at least partly related to a "sense" of what came to be called "Manifest Destiny." This mood was so named after journalist John L. O'Sullivan wrote, in 1845, that nothing should interfere with "the fulfilment of our manifest destiny to overspread the continent allotted by Providence for the free development of our yearly multiplying millions." The problem is that this "overspreading" included slave labor and both betraying and subduing Native Americans and others. See (1) John A. Garraty, *The American Nation: A History of the United States to 1877* (New York: Harper and Row, 1971), 367–69; and (2) Thomas A. Bailey, *A Diplomatic History of the American People* (New York: Apple-Century-Crofts, 1970), 4.

21. One recent attitude among a very few on the radical fringe of political and neo-evangelical circles reflects anarchical characteristics, even espousing violence against the government of the United States which, they argue, has usurped the God-given rights of the people. Timothy McVeigh, who was convicted of bombing the Murrah Federal Building in Oklahoma City in April 1995, is rumored to have had contact with one such group.

22. 1 Peter 2:9–17.

23. Isaiah 2:4.

24. Luke 4:16–21.

25. Mark 1:14–15.

26. Matthew 6:33 and Luke 12:31.

27. Matthew 22:1–10 and Luke 14:15–24.

28. Luke 15:1–10.

29. Luke 15:11–32.

30. Luke 4:18, paraphrasing from Isaiah 42:7.

31. Isaiah 61:2 and Matthew 5:4.

32. Revelation 20:10.

33. Isaiah 25:8; 35:10; and Revelation 21:4.

CHAPTER 7. DO PRESBYTERIANS HAVE SPIRIT, OR DO THEY JUST DRINK THEM?

1. We should be clear that, in discussing the issue of speaking in tongues, what we generally are calling "the neo-evangelical tradition" is far from agreement on that issue. The Pentecostal Christians understand speaking in tongues as one essential part to the life of the church. Churches more identified with fundamentalism, in contrast, have great suspicion about speaking in tongues as an expression of the faith. This illustrates the difficulty in assuming a uniformity among neo-evangelicals that simply does not exist "across the board" when identifying beliefs, practices, or issues. Some neo-evangelicals are also neo-Pentecostals and others are anti-Pentecostal.

2. Jesus quoting Deuteronomy 6:5 and Leviticus 19:18, noted in the Gospel accounts at Mark 12:28–31; Matthew 22:35–39; and Luke 10:27.

3. Acts 2:13.

4. Many preachers and evangelists among neo-evangelicals (both fundamentalists and neo-Pentecostals) at times measure the success of their worship leadership by how many "souls were saved." Often entire careers are measured by how many people are converted through their respective ministries.

5. Acts 2:1–13.

6. It can be argued that the story of Pentecost with speaking in tongues as described in Acts 2:1–12 is a symbolic story of the Spirit empowering the church to go out into the world and speak the gospel in all languages of the world. Such a gift of the Spirit is for a purpose. That purpose is to help the church witness with words and deeds as God gives understanding in the midst of God's people for the ministry of Christ.

7. See Paul's discussion in 1 Corinthians 14:1–40.

8. There is some basis for a reluctance about applause following a person's talented contribution in worship. When someone, for example, sings a beautiful song that touches any of us deeply, we know this has been done not for our appreciation, but as an act of worship to God. People, according to this perspective, are not performing for us or others in worship. They are performing for God. There is no theological reason why God couldn't express God's appreciation by having us clap

spontaneously, or that we couldn't express thanks to God with our applause, or with saying, "Praise God!" or "Amen!" There's also no theological reason that Presbyterians can't tap their feet and clap to a particularly rhythmic song other than the reason that we're afraid that we may not have rhythm.

9. See *The Constitution of the Presbyterian Church (U.S.A.)*, Part II, *Book of Order*, G-14.0301b. Those ordained as Presbyterian Church (U.S.A.) clergy must have a college undergraduate degree, and then achieve a master's degree at a church-approved seminary. They ordinarily also must demonstrate proficiency in a biblical language and in other areas such as theology, Bible, worship, and church polity.

10. Matthew 6:1–18.

11. New resources from the Presbyterian Publishing Corporation and other church publishing companies have been published recently or are "on the drawing board." These contain both "praise music" and contemplative songs from a variety of contemporary and classical sources and, of course, can be utilized as they correspond to the style and theological perspective of those worshiping with such resources.

12. *Book of Common Worship* (Louisville, Ky.: Westminster/John Knox Press, 1993), 431–88 and 1005–22.

13. The list of such authors with Presbyterian-type backgrounds includes, but is not limited to, Frederick Buechner, Annie Dillard, Kathleen Norris, Eugene Peterson, Howard Rice, and Majorie Thompson.

14. Matthew 17:1–8; Mark 9:2–8; Luke 9:28–36.

15. Matthew 17:14–20; Mark 9:14–20; Luke 9:37–43.

16. Acts 7:58.

17. Obviously a reference to Moses being encountered by God (Genesis 3:1 and verses following), interestingly enough, on a mountaintop.

18. 2 Timothy 1:5–7.

19. It is no coincidence that many call the prayer before each meal, "saying grace."

20. Alice Walker, *The Color Purple* (New York: Simon and Schuster, Inc., 1982), 203.

CHAPTER 8. WHY DON'T YOU REPENT IN DUST AND ASHES?

1. For an excellent presentation on this, see Migliore, *Faith Seeking Understanding*, 120–38.

2. *The Constitution of the Presbyterian Church (U.S.A.)*, Part II, *Book of Order*, G-2.0500(4).

3. Migliore, *Faith Seeking Understanding*, 135.

4. Leith, *John Calvin's Doctrine of the Christian Life*, 69.

5. J. Gerald Janzen, *Job: Interpretation, A Bible Commentary for Teaching and Preaching* (Atlanta: John Knox Press, 1985), 254–59.

6. Geneva Catechism (1541), questions and responses 221 and 222, here quoted from Leith, *John Calvin's Doctrine of the Christian Life,* 185.

CHAPTER 9. WHO'S IN CHARGE?

1. John H. Leith, *An Introduction to the Reformed Tradition: A Way of Being the Christian Community* (Atlanta: John Knox Press, 1977), 153.

2. *The Constitution of the Presbyterian Church (U.S.A.),* Part II, *Book of Order,* G-1.0100.

3. Ibid., G-1.0304.

4. Ibid., G-1.0301 (noting that this is quoted from the Westminster Confession of Faith, *The Constitution of the Presbyterian Church (U.S.A.),* Part I, *Book of Confessions,* 6.109).

5. Ibid., G-1.0307. For further comment on what is necessary and essential for Presbyterian Church officers to believe and acknowledge, and what is open to individual interpretation and disagreement, see (1) Jack Rogers, *Presbyterian Creeds: A Guide to the Book of Confessions* (Philadelphia: Westminster Press, 1985), 22–23; and (2) Jack Rogers, *Reading the Bible and the Confessions: The Presbyterian Way* (Louisville, Ky.: Westerminster John Knox Press, 1999), especially 125–27.

6. Douglas F. Ottati, *Reforming Protestantism* (Louisville, Ky.: Westminster John Knox Press, 1995), 93–116.

7. See Douglas John Hall, *The Steward: A Biblical Symbol Come of Age* (New York: Friendship Press, 1982), 129–40.

8. See especially the careful wording of chapter 16 of the Scots' Confession, *The Constitution of the Presbyterian Church (U.S.A.),* Part I, *Book of Confessions,* 3.16.

9. For an excellent presentation on the perspective, see Guthrie, *Always Being Reformed,* chapters 2, 3, 5, and 6.

10. Migliore, *Faith Seeking Understanding,* 186–88.

11. For what may be the statement without peer of "The Church and Its Mission," see *The Constitution of the Presbyterian Church (U.S.A.),* Part II, *Book of Order,* G-3.0100–3.0400.

12. Presbyterian minister the Reverend George K. Kluber has been heard saying this (as others may have said it) to explain how Presbyterians are convinced God's Spirit is at work in ministry and corporate decision-making processes in church and culture as much as in the lives of individuals. This latter individual aspect is the primary focus of many neo-evangelical and neo-charismatic understandings of the Holy Spirit.

EPILOGUE

1. Genesis 3:6–13.

2. *"Ecclesia reformata, semper reformanda,"* Latin for "The church reformed, always being reformed."